If Only they Knew

HOW TO CREATE A FULL-TIME FREEDOM BUSINESS ON YOUR OWN TERMS

CHICHI ERUCHALU

Copyright © 2017 Chichi Eruchalu
Cover Photograph© Michelle Wildman

All rights reserved. No part of this publication may be reproduced, distributed, or transmitted in any form or including photocopying, recording, or other electronic or mechanical methods, without the prior written permission of the publisher, except in the case of brief quotations embodied in reviews and certain other non-commercial uses permitted by copyright law.

ISBN: 1977752950
ISBN-13: 978-1977752956

Date of publication: October 2017
Published by CE Consulting & Media Limited

www.chichieruchalu.com

To access the bonus training hub to support the book please visit: **http://chichie.co/ifonlytheyknewbook**

Join my free Facebook Community – CEO Mastery
www.ceomasterygroup.com

To my children Siobi and Chizobe, who completely changed my life around for the better, you both are my source of constant inspiration. I am honoured to be your mother.

To the whole CEO Mastery Community who remind me that anything and everything is possible, if you believe that it is. Thank you for being part of the journey.

PRAISE FOR CHICHI

It's rare that you come across standout talent like Chichi, my only regret is that I had not met her at the beginning of my business journey.

I had followed Chichi for a long time, reading her newsletters, participating in her challenges and generally soaking up all of her amazing coaching work.

Earlier this year I booked a coaching session with her and in such a short time she was able to help me stop procrastinating and put my ideas into action. I am in awe of Chichi's ability to get to the nub of a problem and provide several solutions.

If you are an entrepreneur or business owner looking for a coach to help move you and your business forward, I would highly recommend Chichi.
Michelle Gymiah - Equality Pays

***

Chichi you have been a huge part of my business journey and I know 100% I wouldn't be where I am right now if it wasn't for you. Your belief in me and ongoing guidance and support is so appreciated.

I've been lucky enough to see how you run your business from behind the scenes and it's beautiful to see that what you show in the outside is who you are behind the scenes too.

You are such a heart centered coach, and have a genuine desire to help everyone!
You've taught me so much and helped me in my business and in my personal growth, so thank you!!
Deborah Farquhar - Life Esteem

***

Private mentoring with Chichi propelled my business forward to a new, unexpected level.
Chichi opened my eyes to what else is possible for my business and with this new vision in mind, I was able to create a whole new income stream that although the possibility had always been there, I had never seen it!!

I can feel that Chichi really believes in me and with her guidance, business knowledge and continuous support, my income is increasing consistently. Thank you so much, Chichi!"

Christine Juette - Christine Juette Photography

***

A Big and Heartfelt *"Thank You"* to this amazing business coach Chichi Eruchalu.

It is rare to come across a coach that truly gives and has your success in mind when working with you.

She tells you nothing is magic but with real work and with clarity – knowing who you are, you can truly grow your business. She does not just talk but focuses on you helping you identify how you can be the best for your business with your strengths.

OmozuaIsiramen - Life Coach

ACKNOWLEDGEMENTS

Where do I even start when it comes to saying thank you. I wrote this book in three weeks, but it is the culmination of my entire journey to date.

I thought I knew what to expect going into it, but it turned out to be much bigger than I could ever imagine.

It takes a village to write a book, a *village* and I want to honour my "village" right now.

I want to thank God first. I couldn't do any of this without His daily grace, love, and protection. For the ideas and creativity He pours out to me, for the clients and opportunities He brings my way. I am grateful.

To my team, ToseUmobuarie and Natalia Komis, you are the women behind the woman. You work hard behind the scenes so that I can shine confidently at the front. It is incredible all the things we have accomplished this past year. Thank you for your commitment to the vision and for your hard work in helping to build this global empire!

To my mentor Victor EkpoBassey, my business changed when DJ Sobanjo introduced me to your world. (Thanks

DJ)! At first, I was like "who is this crazy guy?" But your passion, drive and excellence in all that you do were so engaging, it inspired me to hang around and learn more. Since working with you, my business has evolved into something far greater than I could have imagined. You encourage me to play a bigger game, seeing my potential and pushing me to aim higher, even when I'm scared. You provide a listening ear and a sounding board when I need it the most. For your continued guidance, support and dancing emojis, I say thank you. This book, would not have happened without the push from you!

To Joanne Grobblear, I am grateful the day we connected over in *that* group. I always say everyone needs a "Jo" in their life and it's so true. You provide the space for me to be me, a place to get messy, to break everything down and rebuild it back again stronger. You have been my biggest cheerleader and encourager, and I thank you for being there every step of the way.

EmekaNobis, the master writer. I love the way you take words and make them come alive. The Launch Team Strategy was all you, and I put my *"Chichi"* spin on it and made it happen. You are a great mind and I enjoy learning from you. Thank you for supporting my vision for this book and all your encouragement. I am proud to call myself a "writer" under your tutelage.

To my editor, TonyeAdenusi, when I told you we were editing a 32,000-word book in two weeks, you didn't flinch. I am so happy to have worked with you on this. You took my words and made them better, but you also understood the vision of the book and ensured it was never lost. Thank you for all your hard work and folks if you need a copywriter, check her out over at **www.written-copy.co.uk**

ObyBamidele, thank you for your genuine friendship and support. You see me for me and call me out in a way only a real friend can. You are a brilliant mind and a generous soul, thank you for being there on this journey. I appreciate you.

EzinneMeribe, thank you for keeping me accountable. For the late night calls, regular WhatsApp messages and early morning brainstorming sessions. Your help these past few months, especially with the book launch has been invaluable. Thank you.

Lorraine Adebowale, you have been my Chief Encouragement Officer. Always ready to listen and ready to pray. You read the first draft and lovingly challenged me to take it up a notch, and I am grateful that you did. Last year you gifted me your time, and helped craft some of the stories that are in the book today. You see the greatness in others, even when they don't see it themselves and I am blessed to call you a friend. Thank you for never-ending love, support, and feedback!

To NkechiUdoh, you have looked after my children since they were babies. Having you on my team brings so much peace of mind as you love my children as if they were your own. Knowing that they are safe hands, allows me to do what I need to do with ease. Thank you for your constant presence and support in our lives, we appreciate you.

To all the women inside the CEO Mastery Community including all my incredible clients, it because of you this book even exists. You buy my products, watch my videos, listen to my podcasts and comment on my posts. You inspire me to become better every day, and this book is a culmination of everything we have built together. Thank you for being the best community a girl could have. We are changing the world together.

Finally to my husband, Afam Eruchalu. Thank you for showing me that I am worthy of so much more.

FOREWORD

The world has changed quite a bit from when I was much younger.

Back then...if you wanted to start a business the primary consideration was capital. Today it's much different.

The primary consideration today is **COURAGE.**

Do you have the guts to go out and make your entrepreneurial dreams come true?

In a world where a sixteen-year-old girl can start a Facebook group and be profitable in six weeks working on her mobile phone, it's no longer capital that is the doorkeeper to entrepreneurial success…

It's *courage,* and Chichi Eruchalu embodies that courage.

I've worked with Chichi for more than a year, and in that time I've come to respect her as a beautiful, authentic soul who truly walks her talk. I watched her quit a great job with absolutely no guarantees.I've seen her get knocked down by life and the market place.
But she didn't stay down.

She got right back up…got back in the game…and won.

So believe me when I say: *She walks her talk.*

This book is absolutely like Chichi.

Authentic. Bold. Absolutely BS free.

In this amazing book, Chichi not only shares with you her story, but she also shows you exactly how to find and cultivate that courage I talked about earlier. She shows you how to use it as a foundation for creating an amazing business that gives you the freedom to do work you like, how you like, with people you like and where you like. In other words, you'll learn to live life on your own terms as an entrepreneur.

All over the earth, people are waking up to the fact that the world is no longer a very safe place for employees. The idea of a safe, secure job is dead and buried. And gone are the days when you could depend on the government to take care of you.

The world isn't going to take care of you. And neither is the government. You have to do that for yourself, and

Chichi lays out a framework for empowering you to do just that in this book.

Within this book, you'll not only find a system for developing the courage to start a business of your own, but also an authentic teacher committed to showing you how to create freedom for yourself by becoming an entrepreneur.

Whether you're interested in starting a business full-time, part-time, in-between time - anytime, this book shows you how to do that successfully and on your own terms.

Jean-Baptiste Say - the French economist - had a definition for entrepreneurship that I have found to be pretty liberating. He said that entrepreneurship is about *moving resources from areas of lower productivity to areas of higher productivity.* In other words, entrepreneurship is about how to best deploy your talents, abilities, time, energy and resources for maximum results.

In this book, you're going to learn how to achieve just that. Sometimes people struggle in business, not because they're doing the wrong things, but because they're doing the right things at the wrong time and for the wrong people.

If Only They Knew helps you gain the clarity you need to do the right thing at the right time and to recognize opportunity when you see it. But it doesn't just stop there. It also helps you develop the courage you need to take advantage of an identified opportunity and the capability to leverage it effectively.

I encourage you to do more than just read this book. I urge you to live it. Take action on it every single day, and one day, you'll wake up in the morning and realize that life and the marketplace have gifted you with a potent and precious gift.

The gift of **freedom.**

Victor EkpoBassey

Co-founder, The Highly Paid Experts Network

CONTENTS

Introduction 1
If Only They Knew 4
How To Use This Book 6

SECTION ONE: MY JOURNEY SO FAR 9

Stop Hiding 10
Your life. Your terms. 13
My Story 16
Success + Mission 32
When things are not working and you need to PIVOT 37

SECTION TWO: THE CEO MASTERY FRAMEWORK 52

Define The Vision 54
Discover Your Genius Power 59
Develop The CEO Mindset 69
Design To Win 76
Getting started: Tips for Service-Based Entrepreneurs 81
Delegate To Dominate 86

SECTION 3: RUNNING YOUR BUSINESS 95

Be Intentional 96
Invest In The Right Tools 98
Create The Right Environment 100
Build Your Systems 101
Get Yourself Covered Legally 106
Planning Tips 107

Getting Clients 109
My Journey To Fully Booked 113
Choosing Faith Over Fear 115
Staying The Course When You Feel Like Quitting......117
"Kaizen" - The Art Of Continuous Improvement 121
Sowing Seeds 127
Pushing or Pulling? 129
Be vs Do - What got you here isn't going to get you there..133
'Future You' Decisions..134
Not Settling..135
Investing In Yourself 138
Measuring Growth - The Three Cs 141
Feeling Lonely 143
No woman is an island 144
Weekday Warriors - For All my 9-5 Hustlers...............148

SECTION FOUR: THE CONSISTENCY QUADRANT 160
Staying Consistent...161
Mindset + Confidence 172
Visibility and Community...193
Systems - Building a Virtual Team or Outsourcing.....211
Money Mastery 221

FINAL THOUGHTS 228
23 Business Lessons - Things I Have Learnt.................229
Final Words - Note from Chichi 232

Enjoyed the book	234
The Collective	236
About The Author	240
Let's Connect	242
References	243

INTRODUCTION

Just over a year ago, I walked away from my corporate 9-5 job to become a full-time entrepreneur, stepping into an incredible business which has brought so much fulfilment into my life.

Today I run a global business on my own terms and in the best way to support myself, my lifestyle, my family, and goals. I focus on the 20% which gets me the 80% impact. But it wasn't always that way.

I have been in the online space for over five years now, and in July 2015, I reached burnout.

I had returned to work as a Project Manager in May after maternity leave, my husband was working abroad, and I was trying to run my business with a new job and two kids under the age of 5. It wasn't pretty.

I was doing "all the things", listening to too many people, buying too many courses and not trusting myself.
The result – I ended up frustrated, overwhelmed and broke. My confidence was at an all-time low (as was my bank balance) and my mindset was all wrong.
I stopped believing in myself.

I decided to step away from my business and took time to redefine what success looked like for me.

It was in those moments that I realised something. You have to design your life first, and *then* build a business to support it in order to have real full-time freedom, not the other way round, like many of us do.

Today I am thrilled to have a thriving coaching practice as well as lead a 4000+ strong community called **CEO Mastery**, where I empower women around the world to start and grow their own businesses so that they too can create lasting impact and legacy in their lives and the lives of those around them.

I am also the host of the **CEO Mastery Podcast**, CEO Mastery Daily Digest and the founder of **The Collective** and have been published in The Huffington Post, The Guardian and I am a 'Go and Grow Online Advisor' for Enterprise Nation. Earlier this year I also won runner-up in IPSE 2017 Freelancer of the Year Awards.

Besides all this, I'm a daughter, sister to five siblings, wife to one husband and mum to two incredibly smart and adorable children who make the sun shine for me and I'm truly grateful for the lifestyle my business affords me.

I get to do the schools runs and school trips, I can take time off and enjoy the school holidays, and more importantly, I am walking in *my* purpose and showing my children that anything is possible. I'm an imperfect woman, loved by a perfect God, and that knowledge keeps me strong day after day.

I encourage you to do more than dream. Whatever you want to create in your life, you can do so…if you believe you can.

It happened for me, and there's nothing magical about me. I am a just girl who had a dream and a desire to make it happen.

This is just the beginning.

IF ONLY THEY KNEW

I find online business fascinating. How you can take an idea, put it out to the world and people buy without ever physically meeting you. And now with the power of the Internet, you have an instant global marketplace.

You have an opportunity to change your life and the lives of those around you, all with minimal upfront cost. It is incredible.

This book takes you on my journey of entrepreneurship and how I went from the corporate cubicle to virtual assistant, then web designer and now award-winning Consultant, Speaker, Author, and Coach. It's less about the steps and more about the lessons I learnt along the way. The self-discovery and the tools I now use to help hundreds of other women like you, do the same.

I don't believe in coincidences; I'm convinced that things come into our lives at the exact moment we need them.

I am thrilled that you are reading this book, because - as the saying goes - *"when the student is ready the teacher appears."* So today I thank you for being a willing student.

If Only They Knew shares the many lessons, I have learnt while building the business I have today. And the frameworks I created to help my clients do the same and the things you need to aware of as an entrepreneur.

If you know me, you know I like to keep it real, and this book is no different. I won't be sugar-coating things because it doesn't help you or help me. I won't be "keeping all the secrets" either, because I want to see you succeed and if this book enables you to do that, then fantastic!

Now I know some of you will devour this book and go and take immediate action. Others will read it and then let it gather dust on your digital bookshelf. I encourage you to commit to taking action, as that is the only way you will see results.

I also trust and pray that you will be blessed, inspired and encouraged to keep going, and to create the very best life for yourself, one that impacts many for generations to come.

HOW TO USE THIS BOOK

My aim for this book is to help you create the foundations for your own full-time freedom business. To help you get clarity on the things you want in your life and to take steps to build a business that will help you achieve that. To know that the entrepreneurial journey, while it has its ups and downs is FUN and hugely rewarding.

This book is split into four sections:
- My Journey So Far
- The CEO Mastery Framework for Designing your Full-Time Freedom Business
- Getting Started and Running Your Business
- The Consistency Quadrant for Long-term Success

It's my blueprint of the things that I did (and still do), and I don't want you to feel like you need to copy every strategy and tactic line-for-line because you are not me. I do however want you to look at what I did and ask yourself, what aspects could work for me and my business?

Throughout the chapters, you will see actions points which is your opportunity to reflect and ask yourself, "What does this mean for me? How can I apply this?"Believe me, there is nothing worse consuming this book and then taking no action.

I have also created a resource hub to support the book, where you can download some additional bonuses as well as some worksheets and templates.

You can access that here:
http://chichie.co/ifonlytheyknewbook.

Alright, let's do this!

SECTION ONE: MY JOURNEY SO FAR

STOP HIDING

You are a leader
A trailblazer
A warrior

You thought your dreams were no longer possible, but something inside of you has awoken.

The passion
The desire
The drive to make a difference
To make a greater impact
Not just in YOUR life but in the lives of those around you

The realisation that it is time.

Time to stop settling
Time to stop making excuses
Time to start pushing

Pushing at the edges of fear
Pushing away at society views
Pushing away at cultural expectations

Stepping into the woman you know you were called to be.

To be the voice, where there are no voices
To lead with courage and be fearless
To care less about what others think, show up and share your message
To shut out the noise and get focused
To want it bad enough

Because through it all, you know this is what you want.

I am so passionate about helping you create this because I see you. You show up every day, taking action, learning, making changes and pushing yourself forward in your business. You're doing all the "right" things but are not seeing the results you know you should.

You are BRILLIANT at what you do, and now it is time for the rest of the world to see that.
Business success is simple, and to create the life you want starts with intention.

Intention then action.

Surrounding yourself with high-calibre people who will elevate you more than you know, and knowing that "someone has your back".

I urge you to stop making excuses.

Stop saying that you're not good enough - looking around and comparing because you are enough. *You can do this.*

Take off your mask and stop hiding - the world is waiting to hear from you.

Welcome to CEO Mastery.

YOUR LIFE. YOUR TERMS.

CREATING A BUSINESS ON YOUR OWN TERMS

Friday, January 29th, 2017, Facebook:

This past weekend was rather busy, as we were hosting my daughter's birthday party and then I finally got around to doing my taxes.

Given that the tax year ended in April and technically I have had since then to submit my self-assessment, it has been one big procrastination exercise. I wasn't very good at managing my business finances back then, and so the thought of trawling through PayPal, Stripe, the bank account and more pulling out income and expenditure details filled me with dread.

As I sat there inputting numbers, I realised the importance of tracking your money and knowing your financial position, and how empowering it is to do so.

In doing my numbers for that year, it did bring up some weird feelings and emotions.

That was the year when things were not working, and no matter what I did I remained stuck and confused. When things felt like I was pushing rocks up a hill, every single day. A year where I lacked so much self-trust and self-belief, that I poured money into coaches and programs in order for someone to tell me what I needed to do and who I was meant to be - it was crippling.

Did it work? No.

If you know the story, I ended up walking away from my business indefinitely, disconnecting from social media, and going back to God for direction and guidance.

At the time I didn't know if I was going to be back, but I knew that I couldn't continue the same way.
They say everything we need is inside of us, and I don't disagree, but you need to be patient to allow it to come out. What resulted was six weeks of going inward and looking forward.
When I decided "quit" I had no plans. I didn't even think I was coming back. However, the time away gave me much needed clarity, making me realise that YES I was on the right path, but NO I was doing it all wrong.

The lessons that I took away from that period were that you need to design your life and get clear on what you truly want. From there you can create a business to support it.

Does your business do that for you or are you trying to fit your life into your business? Copying what everyone else is doing and getting frustrated?

The online space is really noisy, and you need to know yourself, and what you stand for, otherwise you will get swayed in the wrong direction. You'll find that two experts from the same industry can give conflicting advice and it's hard to know who to listen to. You must be sure of your values, what you stand for and your identity, and work daily to ensure that you don't get lost in the comparison trap or the "not good enough" syndrome.

Define what success looks like and work to stay in your lane to achieve it.

MY STORY

I have always been an entrepreneur.

Even when I was little and my mum would visit the cash and carry, I would ask her to buy me sweets and chocolates in bulk so that I could resell them for a profit to my brothers and sisters.

As I grew into my teenage years, my fascination with technology also grew. This was before the Internet and mobile phones were accessible or affordable. I don't remember getting my first phone until I was about 16 years old. I had managed to collect enough diet coke can tops to exchange for a brick-like handset with the mobile phone company, T-Mobile and I was super excited to get my very first mobile phone.

From that, I upgraded to the legendary Nokia 3210, in the days of changing fascias and polyphonic ringtones. Anyone under the age of 21 reading this will be like, *"what the...?!"* but trust me, it was a big deal back then.

I remember entering 6th Form as a bright and enthusiastic 17-year old. I loved all things business and adored my business and economics teacher, Miss Hall, who nurtured that passion and desire inside of me.

When I told her I wanted to create a beauty line for women of colour - because I was so frustrated going into the drugstore and finding nothing for me - she didn't laugh. She brought me articles and information about starting a cosmetic line.

When I then told her I wanted to create a shoe line - because at the age of 17, I had size 10 feet, and the Kickers line which all my friends were wearing stopped at size 8 - again she encouraged me and sent me links to sites I could read and research more. I remain grateful to Miss Hall for her unwavering belief in me and her desire to nurture those entrepreneurial dreams I had.

Fast forward ten years and I was working as a Project Manager for one of the largest banks in the UK, getting ready to have my first child. The job was fine, but I knew it wasn't my final destination.

I am an 'analytical creative', meaning that while I love spreadsheets and plans, I also love me some Photoshop and WordPress. At the time, I was bored because I wasn't using my creative skills. However, I knew how to play the corporate game - I worked hard and ended the year a top performer, but still unfulfilled and searching for more.

When I left for my maternity leave, I started to explore what I could do that would help me finally leave the corporate world for good and allow me to work for myself.

When I assessed my skills, I realised that all the summers spent working for my dad in his print and design studio had not been in vain. I came across a book called The Bootstrap VA by Lisa Morosky which opened my eyes to another world.

Thoughts like *"You mean to tell me that I can earn money from my laptop? That I can have clients across the world through the power of the internet? That I can create a business from the comfort of my own home and be with my daughter?"*

I was excited by the prospect and soaked it all in. I Googled. I read blogs and absorbed as much as I could to help me get started. I'm extreme like that. If there is something I am interested in, I go deep.

It was then that I first became aware of how powerful the internet was for creating a full-time freedom business. I was seeing women all over the world building successful blogs and Etsy sites.

I began offering my services to people - first design, admin, tech, and then design again. I soon learnt what I loved to do and the kind of clients I wanted to work with, having had a few that weren't a great fit.
I learnt that correctly pricing yourself is critical if you don't want to be stuck two days before Christmas designing 20 different sets of memes at £25 a pop. #truestory.

And just because someone can pay, it doesn't mean you want to take their money and work with them.

I discovered other entrepreneurs online and started working with a business coach in a group program and began to shape my business. I started to make money, and I was excited.

The following year I decided it was time to fine-tune my services because I was tired of the haphazard way in which I was working. I wanted to 'niche down' so that I could become better in particular skills and in time become known for said skills.

I loved graphic design and websites. Being the web designer/developer I was, I grew a successful web-design business, helping other entrepreneurs launch themselves online. I found it easy to learn new things and translate complicated methods into simple steps that people could understand and so that attracted people into my world.

As time progressed, I realised that doing this type of business on my own was not scalable. If I didn't work, I didn't earn. Plus I was capped at how many people I could serve at any one time, and that bothered me.

It was at this point I decided to create my very first course - Creative Web School - teaching people how to design and build their websites across a 4-week period (back then it was a bit harder to pull a website together, especially if you had no experience).

I remember it was my birthday when the idea for the course came to me, and within an hour I had mapped out the modules and shared it with my mastermind group with excitement.

I set about creating my launch campaign, webinar and promotions material for Facebook all without overthinking it but enjoying the excitement that was being created from pulling it all together.

At the same time, I was nervous, thinking to myself, *"what if no one buys this thing?"*

Luckily, I had learnt from my mentor not to build a damn thing until people had put down cash - basically validate the idea first. And I still use this principle today.

I planned my webinar and prepared my slides. I had spent ages researching the best technology options, and I knew from watching the experiences of my peers that it was a rite of passage to experience tech issues on the day, but I prayed about it and trusted it would all be okay.

The day of my webinar came, and in the hour leading up to the start time, my heart was racing, and my mind was spinning, *"I am not ready," "Maybe the slides are not detailed enough," "What if people hate it?"* I took a deep breath, hit 'BROADCAST' and anxiously waited for people to turn up.

To my surprise, over 25 people turned up live, and the webinar ran perfectly with no hitches. I shared all that I knew about web design and at the end, did my very first pitch, inviting them to come and join me in my new course. Phew, I was done! I was no longer a webinar virgin!

I came off the webinar and waited.

An email notification came through -*"You have a sale."* Then another, and then another. To my amazement, ten people signed up to my new course that week. Shocked and in awe, I quickly scrambled to get to work creating the content.

As I had pre-sold the course, no content was created, and so I began to get to work pulling it all together. I grossly underestimated how much time and effort went into creating a course, especially with a toddler and it was the toughest 4-6 weeks of my life, but worth it because I now had an asset that I could sell over and over.

This was my first taste of freedom because now if someone asked about my web design service and I was full or outside of budget, I could now direct them to my course. Result!

My eyes were now open.

Lessons from this experience:
- Pre-sell always
- Give yourself enough time to create (you can never over plan or over-estimate how much time you will need)
- Believe in yourself

As time progressed, people started asking me how they could grow their businesses online and get more clients, I transitioned into business strategy and coaching, with the core focus being visibility. Ironically, I was on my own visibility journey, and they say we teach others what we need to learn ourselves and I was learning.

Contrary to how I may appear online, I am an incredibly shy person and an introvert (INFP for all you Myers Briggs/Personality tests fans). I *love* my own company, and even though I enjoy speaking and training, I find big crowds can be very draining.

At the time of transitioning my business from a 'done-for-you' tangible service to business coaching, I had to overcome my fears around being seen. I lacked the confidence to show up and be me; I felt that I wasn't good enough, the way I was. At the time, I was in a lot of debt and felt embarrassed and ashamed to let people know that about me.

On the outside, I had a good job, a house, a car and nice lifestyle, but behind the scenes, I was drowning in debt to the tune of around £47k.

I was full of shame, and as a result, I did not let people come close to me, putting up barriers to protect myself. When I knew that I could no longer hide behind my laptop and I had to be visible as a coach to position and sell my brand, I was terrified.

I felt because I had made poor decisions with my finances it disqualified me from helping others, and so I didn't trust myself. I didn't believe I was qualified enough and continued to invest in course after course, mentor after mentor. Not because I needed the training but because I felt it was going to be the magic pill and the answer to all my problems. It wasn't.

So many of you are in this same space. You think you have to have everything together before you can be effective or help someone else. This is not true. One major thing I've learnt over time with my clients is that I can give you all the strategies in the world, but if you have things holding you back from actually putting yourself out there, you *will* hold yourself back.

Equally, you don't need to be perfect to make an impact; you just need to be a few steps ahead and be the best version of yourself, today.

Wednesday, July 22, 2015; Facebook:

This time last year I was completely okay to sit behind my laptop screen and expect that new business would fall into my lap. Dumb, right?

I was afraid to be seen, to show my face and claim my expertise and my business numbers reflected this. I wouldn't say or share anything because I didn't want to offend anyone.

I was afraid people wouldn't like me, or I would be seen as a fraud. I had a lot of shame around the debt I was in and didn't want people to know the 'real' me. I didn't believe anyone wanted to hear from me and found it impossible to write even a simple blog post.

I was in hiding and honestly didn't know who I was anymore. The result? A mediocre and lukewarm message that attracted NO ONE.

Why? Because I didn't believe in myself or my message. I didn't feel I deserved it. That realisation meant I had to make changes if I wanted to succeed and so began my journey…

I had to get real with myself, face my fears and learn to forgive myself.

I began to own my truth and share it. Layer by layer, I began to show more of me - **the real unapologetic me** *- and oh my goodness - the freedom I found!*

More to the point, my freedom empowered other women to become more authentic and unapologetic too. How do I know? Because these same women would send me private messages telling me how my posts really spoke to and inspired them.

WHAT! Me?

Yes me. I stopped doubting myself and followed my heart when it came to creating. I stopped listening to voices that were not in alignment. I pushed the fear away and began to trust myself. In return, life became simple and 'Shine and Be Seen' became my new manifesto.

Are you feeling scared to be seen? Don't be. It's okay to ditch the mask and be you.

— —-

It's true; we *do* teach the lessons that we need to learn ourselves. I had to face myself and forgive myself before I could step out boldly and help others.

Was it easy? No. But was it worth it? Oh yes!

— — — — — — — — —

Sunday, June 5th, 2016; Facebook:

STOP HIDING

We teach what we need to learn.

Ladies, I have been hiding in more ways than you know. I was hiding, but I'm playing a bigger game now. And I am calling you in to play a bigger game too.

You are going to see me in more ways, whether it's video, interviews or an unapologetic post. I'm not hiding anymore, and I require everyone reading this to stop hiding too...whatever that means to you because here's the thing: you're NEVER going to get what you want by hiding. By ignoring what you really want instead of going after it. By staying scared and making excuses.

We all get scared - the difference is, being the leader you are, you PUSH past it, and you show up anyway.

So, why have I been hiding?

I have been hiding because I have a corporate job which I haven't left (I've had clients leave their jobs before me), but guess what? I still have clients and regularly have months where my business income exceeds my corporate one.

I have BIG goals.

Some that I have achieved (like buying our house) and others that are on their way (repaying my personal debt).

I am not prepared to leave my job only to return in six months, or run my business from a place of desperation, which is what happens when you're scrambling for cash each month to pay basic bills, much less invest in your business. I am not prepared to jeopardise the day-to-day well being of my family, if I don't have to, or leave a full-time job, only to enter another self-imposed one.

For me, this is a marathon, not a sprint, and so I'm taking time to build a business with a very strong foundation. One that I can scale and leave at the right time.

Plus having that stability allows me then to reinvest into my business and work with the best, mentors and coaches in my industry.

I am not scared to invest and I do it with ease. Success is different for everyone, and for me I know what I'm building and the life I'm creating. I don't apologise for it anymore and I don't work with anyone who passes judgement on that.

So here's the bottom line, if I can still SHOW UP in my business EVERY SINGLE DAY with a full-time job, a 4-year old and a 22-month old...what's your excuse?

Time to stop hiding.

#excusesstophere

Running a business is probably one of the most significant self-development tools out there. It forces you to get clear on who you are and what you believe.

You have to commit to showing up and doing the necessary work, whether you feel like it or not. The online space especially likes to paint a glossy lifestyle - photographs in Paris in front of the Eiffel Tower, flashy cars and laptops on the beach - like you can achieve all of this overnight.

It isn't true. It's hard work, sacrifice but ultimately if you don't give up, it pays off every time, and you can create the life, *you* want for yourself.

SUCCESS + MISSION

WHAT IS YOUR MISSION?

What is it that you are called to do? What is the thing that you can spend *hours on*, and time seems to stand still? The thing that you would do for free if you could?

Why are you here? *That* is the question *you* need to answer. If you already have your answer, I applaud you, because many others don't.

My mission is to empower women globally to stop hiding. To start and grow successful businesses that allow you to create wealth, freedom, and impact in your life and the lives of those around you.

Why? Because there is nothing worse than having a gift and never unwrapping it, which is why I am:

- **Passionate** about all women having a voice and talking about the issues that actually matter
- **Determined** to understand different cultures and ways of thinking so that I can approach things from a place of understanding and not ignorance

- **Intent** on teaching you that it is easy to become self-sufficient and not have to rely on the state, or friends and family. God has blessed you with gifts. You can take your skills and, through the power of the internet, create a full-time income for yourself and then, in turn, impact your family, your community, and the world
- **Focused** on forging my own path, the only competition is with myself
- **Showing** the next generation what is possible and stepping outside of comfort zone daily
- **Leading** by example
- Not going to stand for laziness, excuses and pity parties. We have all been born into an amazing time in society. Resources and opportunities abound. If you waste it, it's on you.

"If you are born poor its not your mistake, But if you die poor its your mistake."Bill Gates

So, what *is* your mission? And *why* are you doing whatever it is that you're doing? What does success look like for you?

I used to think it was all about the money. That once I hit £10k, life would be perfect, but I hit my first £10k month, and (to my surprise) life continued as usual. Nothing really changed, and it was then that I was reminded that success runs deeper than money.

It's really easy to look around at what others are doing and want to copy them - to copy *their* version of success. But that's the worst thing you can do. Because you will likely find that you've climbed up a ladder only to realise at the top, that it's leaning against the wrong wall.

You have to define what success means to *you* - ask yourself what is it that makes you truly happy and fulfilled. *Is it your family? Or maybe it's freedom to travel? The opportunity to give back and support others?* Whatever it is, get clear on that *first* and then define your success metrics.

Success for me means freedom to be myself, do the things I love, and make a lasting impact. It's waking up excited to get to work (#lovemondays).

It's working to create a family environment that honours God and raises leaders, and hanging out with my minis whenever I choose. Success is great relationships, and being able to fail, pick myself up and carry on. Success, for me, is leading by example.

Now it's your turn. **What's *your* version of success? Write it down.**

WHY ARE YOU IN BUSINESS?

Now that you're clear on what a successful life looks like for you let's delve a little deeper. What are your reasons for being in business? Or if you don't have a business yet, why do you want to be in business?

This is such a powerful question because it will drive all your actions from here on out. What is it that calls you into the world of entrepreneurship? Do you want: *More money? More freedom? To travel more? To simply have more time to do whatever you need?*

For me, aside from the obvious of earning my own income and having freedom, my core desire for having my business is the ability to impact and empower others.

There is something amazing which happens when you help someone get the clarity they need. To take the steps that will change their life forever.
When you teach them the strategy and give them the tools, and you see them taking action and making progress. Nothing brings me more joy than this.

I have always had a deep desire to help women recognise their potential, unlock it, monetise it and use their wealth to make a lasting impact, not only in their lives but the lives of their family and community too. So that is my "why".

Get clear on *why* you are doing this. It *cannot* just be about money; it has to run deeper.

WHEN THINGS ARE NOT WORKING AND YOU NEED TO PIVOT

Alright, let's talk about business and the reality of business.

Running a business is hard work. I'm not going to lie. Anybody who tells you it's a walk in the park is lying to you. Your business requires you to sacrifice. It requires you to show up every day. It requires you to be 100% 'in' because if you want to have a successful business, you cannot approach it with the mindset of "it's a hobby."

With that in mind, it's important to remember that business should also be fun. You should enjoy what you do.

Yes, it's hard work, but I genuinely love my business. I love what I do, and the clients I serve. For me, although it's not a walk in the park, it never feels like 'work' because I *really* enjoy what I do.

If you start to see signs that you've stopped enjoying your business - you resent your clients, you're frustrated all the time, and everything feels like an uphill task - that's a sign for you to step back and reflect on what you're doing.

Ask yourself, *"Is my business going in the right direction? Am I doing the right thing? Do I need to take a step back and review? What is out of alignment?"*

That's precisely how I felt for most of 2015.

I was busy trying to do so many different things without having a clear focus as to what I was doing. I was building my coaching business alongside my VA business, and trying to get it off the ground, but I lacked focus and clarity.

I was quite disorganised about it and had no clear strategy for maximising my efforts. I was buying lots of different programmes, hanging out in different Facebook groups and not really taking the right action that I needed to see my business grow.

I hated sales, so I didn't do any.

I wasn't really clear on who I was helping, even though I knew I could help people.
I was juggling the demands of two young children with a 3-hour daily commute and a demanding job while running my household while my husband worked in a different country during the week. If you factor into the

mix trying to get a new business off the ground, you can just imagine what life was like.

It was horrible.

I was exhausted. I felt frustrated and confused.

I tried to manage it all, but it just wasn't working. My approach was all wrong. If I could do it all over again, I would do so many things differently, particularly in how I supported myself, both personally and in my business.

At the time I was hardly sleeping, eating or being a productive member of society and I knew something had to give. I'd gone back to work in May, and by July, I thought *"I can't do this anymore,"* so I walked away from my business.

As the popular saying goes, you don't know what you don't know - and I didn't know much! At the time, I had no idea about what I was going to do. I didn't know what walking away would mean for me, I just knew that I had to get away from my business for a little while to think and regroup.

In that time, I disconnected myself from social media, became friends again with my journal and spent time asking myself the questions that really mattered because I created the space to do so.

Regular time and space to think is something that, as women who Consistently Execute at every Opportunity (CEOs), we should have on a regular basis. It's something that I factor into my life now - taking what I call a 'CEO day,' where I plan, strategise, reflect and ask myself, *"What's working right now in the business? What do I need to change?"*

If you don't have the time to think and the head-space to analyse the answers to those questions, it will be difficult for you to know how to move forward. Too many of us are 'go-go-go!' because we are afraid to slow down and stop.

I urge you to give yourself the gift of space.

That much-needed space is precisely what I got during my six-week hiatus. I had to answer my own questions, about what my big vision looked like, and what exactly I was trying to create for my life. I always say, *"It's **your** life. What are you trying to create? What kind of life do you want?"*

Answer those questions, and then you can really move forward and design a business that supports your goals.

Having identified my big vision and my limitations, I realised a few things. Firstly I needed to leverage my time as much as possible; I was doing things that I should have been outsourcing. Secondly, I needed to employ better boundaries in my business and get better support. The constant chasing of my tail had to stop and I had to begin to trust myself.

Know that in business there will be different kinds of struggles. There's the kind that arecentred around, *"I'm new in business and I'm struggling, even though it's early days,"* or there's *"I've been in business for a year. I haven't had a single client. I'm not making any money"*.

Whatever the scenario, the bottom line is, if you find yourself always in that state of perpetual struggle, then something is off.

You need to sit down with yourself and ask, "*Where am I going wrong?*" and answer honestly. Get help if you're not sure. Otherwise, you will find yourself getting increasingly frustrated while pouring more and more money and time into your business for very little return.

For me, I got to a point where I couldn't even think for myself anymore. If I wanted to make a decision, I would go and crowdsource it on Facebook and get so many different people's opinions that I became more confused, before I could decide what I wanted to do. It was just ridiculous.

If you've lost the sense of fun and adventure in your business, or have become disconnected from your message and what you're doing, you need to stop and take stock. There are things that we are passionate about, but they are not necessarily things that we are going to build a business around.

It's really about feeling aligned to what you're doing in your business - this remains a big thing for me.

When you find yourself struggling within your business, it's because something is not in alignment.

Your heart, passions, and purpose should work together to make your business flow. It should be natural, an extension of you.

Of course, as I said before, it *is* hard work. You have got to do the work, but it shouldn't feel unnatural or uncomfortable all the time. You must repeatedly check in with yourself and ask, "*How do I feel? What is it that I want to feel?*" And if there's a gap, ask "*How can I close that gap?*"

I was able to redesign my business from the ground up, focusing on making sure I did things that were centered around my strengths but also gave me the freedom to live the life I wanted.

Now some of you may be thinking, "I just don't like my business anymore," even though it's earning you money. It is okay to review your business choices and ask yourself, "*Why is that*?". It could be that you need to have better boundaries, look for a different type of customer or change the work that you're doing. Be open to the different opportunities.

When I first started as a Virtual Assistant, I was doing admin and data-entry, and I soon discovered that I hated that type of work. That is not my zone of genius and is not what I excel in. I was earning money from it, but I was thinking, "*I hate this. Please do not give me another MailChimp spreadsheet ever again!*"

Be sure to keep asking yourself, *"What is it that really excites me and lights me up?"*

If it's not what you're doing right now, then you need to change that because entrepreneurship is a *choice*. Nobody has forced you into this. You get to choose what you're going to do and how you're going to do it.

You should be enjoying your business, so check in regularly that you're still connected to your bigger mission and why, and your business model supports that.

If you are doing all the necessary things to grow your business, without seeing any results, and it's been like that for a consistent period, again that's another sign for you to ask yourself, *"What's going on here? Do I need to revisit things? Do I need to change things up?"*

I see many people who are stuck in a rut, unfulfilled and unhappy, but who are doing absolutely nothing about it - don't let that be you. Don't be afraid to **PIVOT**, as Julie Stoianoften says.

Another thing that I see people doing is that they take action, get results and rather than say to themselves,

"Wow, that was just amazing, that worked. Let me do more of that," they do the opposite and be like *"Okay! On to the next thing!"*

Why is that?

We don't we do more of what's working. Instead, we put it to one side and start something new. For some of you right now, that revenue increase you are looking for sits in products and services you already have. Dust them off and get them back out to the market.

What are you attracting?

Are you attracting rubbish situations into your life? Rubbish clients, rubbish projects? I believe that we invite the very things that we put out ourselves, so if you're having this negative experience right now, stop for a minute and check where else in your life you are showing up in that way.

You might be someone else's nightmare, which is why you're attracting the wrong situations for yourself. When I discovered this, it gave me real food for thought and highlighted areas where I needed to change and improve.

Stop worrying about what others think

Imagine if we lived in a world where we made decisions without a thought about what others would think. It would be incredibly liberating, right?

Why are we so afraid to stop and change things when we need to? One reason. The opinions of others. Simple as that.

We think, *"Oh, my goodness, I'm going to be seen as a failure. What about all this goodwill and following that I've built up! What will X say?"*

Let me tell you this. It is so much quicker to build a following, to earn money and to make the bigger impact when you are walking in alignment with your purpose, vision and values.

When you are doing something that you shouldn't be doing, or you no longer feel connected to it, everything is much harder.

A simple example - when I was rebranding from Kanso Creative to Chichi Eruchalu (my personal brand), I thought, *"Okay, I need to change my business pages on Facebook."* Then I spent time stressing about, *"Oh, should I change it? It's got 700 'likes' - I can't just change it. I don't want to lose all the likes."*

But the truth is the Kanso Creative page had been with me from the beginning, and the people who had "liked"it, were no longer fully representative of the work and direction I wanted to go in. So I chose to start again so that I could call in and attract those women who I really want to work with.

The result? It took me a fraction of the time to get up to almost 3000 'likes' based on just talking to my ideal client and speaking her language.

Things will move much faster, when you stay in alignment.

Darren L. Johnson (author of *Letting go of Stuff*) said *"In order to grow you need to let go,"* and I agree. Now some people will think, *"But I'm going to have to start again"* and in a practical sense, it's true. You are starting again, but think about how much more knowledge you now have and how quickly you will be able to get from 0 to 100 because you know the steps to get there.

Don't be afraid to pivot if you need to. Your business will thank you for it.

You will thank yourself for it.

Know that it's okay to take a break and give yourself space. If things are not working, take a different approach and see what happens.

Don't keep 'beating a dead horse' just because you don't want to be seen as a failure. I think it's more of a failure to keep pushing something that you know is not working when you could do something else.

Coming Back

So, what happens when you do decide to come back with a new business, a new vision, a new mindset?

You might be feeling excited but unsure of the reaction you will receive. I know I was! Communication here is key. Be sure to bring your clients and your followers along with you, so that they too can understand more about your journey and why you are doing it.

So what happened with me?

During my 6 weeks break, I gained so much more clarity on what my next steps where and what kind of business I wanted to have.

The answer was clear. Design my life first, and my business second.

I realised that I had been doing it all wrong, which is why I was struggling. I was relying on things outside of myself when I had all the resources, skills and things inside of me to do what I needed to do.

I simply needed to learn to trust myself more and make decisions from what I knew to be right, not what other people's opinions were dictating for me.

I said, *"Okay, I want to build this coaching business. I want to work on my own terms. I want to leave my 9-5. I want to be able to have the flexibility and freedom to live life on my terms, and grow a community of women who support and encourage each other."* I was really clear about those things.

I came back to my business around the end of September/early October 2015. That last quarter of the year, I set myself a 100 day goal (thanks Adrienne Dorison for the challenge) of signing up three new one-on-one clients and being able to pay off 10k worth of debt, which I achieved in 10 weeks.

By the 4th December, my third client - my last one of the year - came through. She paid in full, which was incredible and I finished the year on a massive high. I started 2016 refreshed and with a new focus of getting visible and being consistent with it.

With that approach and by making sure I paced myself, I was able to build this beautiful business. I got more support in my personal life and business than ever before. I went from having a 5-hours a month VA to a 10-hours a week VA, and that was a game changer for me.

I explored new things like Facebook advertising. In addition, Facebook Live came out last year, and I thought it was just incredible. I was now doing something that was exciting and fun, and I loved it! Did I mention that I love what I do?

As I said, it's not a 'walk in the park,' it's quite hard work. Of course, it is. But it's done from a place of alignment, and because I'm building this business to support the life that I want, I'm most certainly going to enjoy the process.

I encourage you to be flexible and know that it's alright to change your mind and make decisions to do things differently. I urge you to get fully supported while you do this because often women forget to get support for themselves.

Know that it really is okay to do a 180-degree pivot and switch. It's fine to say, *"This business is not working. I want to do something else"*. You can redefine what your 'awesome' looks like.

And as you grow, your definition of success may change. As you learn more, you might decide *"Actually, I don't want a life like this. Or like that..."* I encourage you to be open. Your life will be all the better for it.

Design your life first. Build your business second.

SECTION TWO:
THE CEO MASTERY FRAMEWORK

In this section of the book, I amgoing to walk you through the CEO Mastery framework which I use for myself and my clients to help design and build a full-time freedom business.

It is broken down into five parts:
1. Define The Vision
2. Discover Your Genius Power
3. Develop The C.E.O. Mindset
4. Design To Win
5. Delegate To Dominate

This framework is foundational because it provides the steps to help you create a business that supports the lifestyle you want, taking into account your dreams, desires, your story and your strengths, and allows you to build a business based on that.

DEFINE THE VISION

What Do You Want?

When I took time away from my business, the first question I asked myself was *"Chichi what do you want?"*

As I began to write down my answers, I sobbed. As simple as this question is, I had never asked it of myself, and it was very empowering. For so long, I had done what others had wanted - go to school, go to university, get a job, buy a house, get married, have kids... but I now found myself in unknown territory.

As I said before, you can't go on a journey if you don't know where you're going; therefore our starting point always has to be the final destination - what do you want for your life? Too many of us build businesses without thinking about the kind of life we ultimately want to have and end up burning out and resenting the 'prison businesses' we have created.

Below I share some exercises that helped me get clarity on this.

1. This time next year

One exercise that I like to that helps me get clarity on my goals fast is to fast-forward to *this time next year*. Close your eyes and picture yourself 12- months from now. Good. What do you see?

What has happened in your life and business that allows you say *"This was my best year yet!"*?
Write it down. This question helps you open up a lot in understanding what it is you truly desire.

2. Dream Day
Imagine your dream or ideal day. What do you see, feel, hear and smell? What are you doing and what are you wearing? How do you start your day? Where are you living? What activities are you doing? Picture it and get clear. Write it all out. Now think about your current day - what is missing from your life that you want to include to take you closer to your dream day?
Once you have got clarity on this, it is powerful to keep a visual representation of what you want to achieve. Try creating a vision board. Either do this manually - cut out or print off images to stick on a corkboard - or you can use a tool like Pinterest to pull images together.

For tips and ideas on this, just google "how to create a vision board" or check out *Dream it. Pin it. Live it.: Make Vision Boards Work For You by Terri Savelle Foy*, which is a great book that breaks it all down.

In my dream day visualisation, I have a beautiful white home office with fresh flowers on my desk. To bring that vision into today's reality I turned our spare bedroom into that space, complete with white IKEA furniture and weekly fresh tulips. I love working in there!

3. Big Money Question

How much do you want to make?

Some of you know this and others of you don't. Being clear on your money goals (and we talk about money mastery in a later chapter) is crucial as it influences the action you take in your business.

If you are serious about your business, then it needs to be earning money.

Profitability is a different thing, but let's start with money coming in. *How much money do you want to earn?* For some of you it might be an additional £1,000, others £5,000 or even £10,000 per day/week, etc. Know why you want to earn the money you want and look to see how you can grow and stabilise your income.

In short, as Stephen Covey says in his book *'7 Habits of Highly Effective People'*, *"you need to start with the end in mind,"* and go from there.

Action questions:
- What is your vision for your life?
- What does success look like and how will you know when you achieve it?
- Where are you now? Be honest.
- How much are you willing to invest? Time, money, etc.

Once you identify your vision, you can now start to create goals that will help you get there.
Goals keep you focused and accountable and help you track progress.

I like to follow the methodology from the book *'12 Week Year by Brian Moran'* and work in 90-day chunks. Every 12 weeks I take stock, review and re-plan. It gives me enough time to make real progress on projects but is not too long that I get bored and start to slack.

Back in 2016, my big goal was to leave my 9-5 and everything I did that year was filtered through that goal. I became hyper-focused and said "no" to a lot of things because I knew they were not going to bring me closer to achieving it.

It was hard because I am a multi-passionate person, I like to have many things on the go, but I knew I could not get distracted. Each quarter I chose a particular theme, systems, visibility, community building or money mastery and just focused.

The result of my focused activity that year was some real growth in my business. I was consistent with my visibility (daily videos and posts) and content creation. My brand developed to a level where I was selling out my programs, having videos go viral and booking regular speaking engagements. All these things led to me being able to hit my goal to leave my corporate job in October last year.

You must have goals, otherwise you will find yourself drifting.
Where do you want your business to be in 3, 6 and 12 months?

DISCOVER YOUR GENIUS POWER

"You are competition-proof" – Petra Foster

Saturday January 12 2016, Facebook:
LOOKING TO STAND OUT? THEN DO THIS:

Own your story.

Plain and simple. You are your story, and your story is your brand.

Your dream clients will resonate and relate with your brand and want to do business with you.

If you have ever struggled with how to look, talk and feel in the online space (or any space for that matter), thinking that by creating a persona or moulding your image on someone else, was going to work, then you are going about it all wrong.

You can't be successful trying to be something that you are NOT.

You can't grow an empire based on someone else's blueprint. Sure you can use their framework to get a structure, but you can't be them.

You have to be YOU.

That's why it's counterproductive to compare yourself to other people, because the truth is, there is NO competition. I mean think about it, how can there be?

We are all so different. In so many ways.

We each have a story.

Unique experiences and skills which make up our own blueprint and you can't fake that.

For some of us, we have tried everything in our power to forget our story.

We don't want to identify with it.

We want to leave it behind.

But you know what is ironic, it is that very thing we want to hide from which connects people to us.

That gives them permission to own their story, embrace their past and rewrite their future.

For me that is talking about my debts and letting go of the shame; removing the mask and allowing people to get to know the real me as I work through my internal battles of self-worth and insecurity. Being okay with being me.

Remember it's not about you.

So, what are you hiding from?

What is your story?

It's time own it.

Chichi xoxo

#shineandbeseen

Each of us has a story. Now we may not like all the chapters in it, but being able to acknowledge all parts of our story can help us identify trends in our experiences and the lessons we can share with others. It also empowers others to own their story and inspire them to know what is possible for them.

I read somewhere recently that *"you don't have a business problem, you have a personal problem mirrored in your business."* That tells me that business is personal and people want to know about *you*. Just like money, business exposes and amplifies who you already are.

If you think that your market is saturated and that there is too much competition, I challenge you to reframe that thinking, because just by the very virtue of you being you, all competition is eliminated.

I remember one of my mentors telling me that I was "competition-proof" and I agree. Even if there were somebody else out there, doing the same thing as you, it wouldn't be the same.

Growing up, I was a shy child. I kept to myself, but what I lacked in speaking up (i.e., I never talked unless I had to), I made up forit with intelligence and curiosity.

I remember my dad telling a story of how he found me, at age 5, browsing through a bunch of newspapers one day and looking more and more perplexed. When he asked me what I was looking for, I said *"common sense."* My dad would always talk about how we needed to have common sense and being the inquisitive mind I was, I went looking for it. #everthelearner

I loved reading even to the point of winning prizes in school for taking out the most books in the library (yes, I was that girl) and my curious mind means that I am forever looking at ways to do things better, improve and do more.

Discovering your genius power is all about getting to know you and what you like. Once you can build a business based on your unique gifts - providing a solution to a market that is willing to pay - then you are golden.

What are you good at? What are your gifts? What do you enjoy doing and could do for hours on end, without food and drink and not even notice?

I often joke that if I didn't have children (or other responsibilities), I could spend all my time working in my business because I genuinely love what I do and it doesn't feel like work when I'm doing it.

What am I good at? Well, there are several things:

* I love teaching and speaking - it sparks something inside of me, being able to take my knowledge and share it with you, to inspire you into action;
* I am also a creative person who enjoys web and graphic design, and fiddling about in Illustrator and WordPress brings me so much joy that I could do it for hours on end.

The difference between the two is that while I have monetised both, the second thing is something that I have recently decided to relegate to "hobby" status -, because although I do enjoy it, I don't always want the pressure of client deadlines attached. As a creative though it is important for me to regularly "be creative" and designing gives me that outlet.

Some of you have businesses based on things you enjoy, but shouldn't necessarily be monetised, and you have other things which you adore and wish you could monetise, but don't know how. You know that thing that you love, that comes naturally to you and which you would happily do for free? If you can monetise it (and you more than likely can), you will find fulfilment.

One of my clients is exactly this. She is a natural writer, she writes amazing stories and has a magical way with words that only some are gifted with. She has tried other businesses and done other things, but nothing has lit her up more than when she decided that she was going to be a copywriter. Because that is her gift - her soul calling - and we each have one. What's yours?

Action questions:
* Who are you?
* What is your story?
* What do you love to do?
* What do you hate to do?
* What experiences and skills can you incorporate into your business?

If you are not sure how it all connects, then spend some time reflecting on your life/career journey so far. What particular things stand out, that you are happy sharing about? These are the things that your clients will connect with.

Some parts of my story include:
* Starting a business as a new mum and the struggles I faced while figuring out how to make my business work, get my first client and sale all with a new baby

* Going back to my 9-5 job and hating it; How I changed my mindset, rebuilt my business and left within 18 months
* Experiencing burnout because I was trying to do things like everybody else and then rising from the ashes
* Building a business model that did not support my lifestyle, and how not to do it again.
* Being in debt and overcoming the shame I felt so that I could become more visible and support my clients who are also dealing with debt and building a business
* Building a business around the needs of my young family and learning how to balance all my other commitments and responsibilities

A lot of my clients come to me because they connect with my story, and I regularly attract people into my community who have gone through or are going through something similar. I can help them because I have experienced this.

Today, even with big brands, people love stories, and that is how you will get consumers to connect with your brand - through storytelling. You need to be clear on your values and what you believe so that you can attract the right people who connect with those values. If you pretend or try to be like somebody else, you will attract people who resonate with that persona, and they will not be your real fans.

People usually hide who they are because they are ashamed, embarrassed or worried about what people will think. They don't feel they know enough or they don't feel good enough. As a result, they don't show up, and they don't sell. In fact, they hide their gifts.

If that sounds like you, then there are some things you need to know (#hometruths):

Not everyone will like you.
People WILL judge you.
People will say mean things.

But it's really not about you!

The way people respond to you is often a reflection of what's going on inside for them. You are you, and you are great - embrace it. Don't try to please everyone - it's exhausting - I know (#wornthetshirt).

Finally, for those of you thinking *"But Chichi, I don't have a 'rags to riches' story, my life is pretty ordinary…"* You have a story too. You have experiences, and you have lessons you can share.

Own your uniqueness, go out and shine and be seen.

So, what *is* your genius power?

DEVELOP THE CEO MINDSET

Are you a CEO in your business or do you *think* you are?

Some of you are employees in your own business without even realising it. When I left my corporate job, I was adamant that I didn't want to go from being an employee for someone else to being an employee for myself.

Some signs that you still have an employee mindset:
* You have no vision
* You are not strategic in your thinking or decisions
* You're doing everything yourself and refuse to get help
* You believe that there is nothing you can do to improve negative situations
* You're rushing around, chopping and changing and not seeing things through

A successful CEO is always thinking about the long game

"How will this decision today get me to where I want to be and help me achieve my goals."

Signs that you have a CEO mindset:

* The way you see yourself and think about yourself is positive
* You take action and execute consistently
* You are committed and stay the course
* You make the necessary investments of time and money
* You believe in yourself

Here's the thing, entrepreneurship is not for everyone. Yes, I said it. For some of you reading this, actually having a 9-5 might be the better option for you and that's okay.

But for those of you who know that entrepreneurship is your life path, it's time to stop sitting on the sidelines and jump in with both feet.

It's interesting because for a long time I thought I was all in. I mean I resigned and left my job, could I possibly be any more committed?
But it wasn't until this summer (2017) that I was really tested when an opportunity for an attractive job was placed before me, and all sorts of things started running through my mind. I began to think how good an opportunity this could be, and even considered how to

balance it with my business. But deep down I knew that it wasn't the answer.

It was at that moment I realised that up until this point I had not been 100% '*in*'.

I still had one foot out there, making sure I had 'options' just in case my business didn't work out, and you simply can't be that way. I'm not saying you shouldn't have a safety net, but you have to be sure that you're choosing the path that's right for you.

I had to make up my mind that this was what *I* wanted and would do whatever I needed to, to ensure success.

Entrepreneurship is a choice. So choose to be 'all in'.

INTRODUCING THE CEO MINDSET MATRIX

The C.E.O. Mindset Matrix is something that I came up with as I built my own framework for my business and my clients.

CEO stands for Consistency, Execution, and Opportunity.

Consistency

One big thing that prevents us from being successful in our businesses is a lack of consistency. It's not often a lack of knowledge or talent, but the fact that we don't continue what we've started. We have a microwave mentality where we expect to see results right away, and if we don't, we give up.

You'll find that if you become a consistent person, you will out-perform most of the people in the marketplace that you're hanging out with. People just quit and move onto something else, and they don't give things a chance to marinate and to see results.

Consistency is fundamental. It's about showing up every day; it's about communicating with your tribe and being visible on a regular basis. Whatever that looks like for you. It's about following through on the things that you say you're going to do and building integrity and trust because regularly showing up is what builds trust.

Execution

I remember Adrienne Dorison, one of my mentors telling me how there is no return on investment for ideas, meaning it's important to get yourself out there, taking action. We like to consume information, and if you're somebody who takes a lot of courses, but not any action, then you will find that you're not going to make any progress.

You have to take action. You have to execute - the second part of this CEO mindset is about execution. It's about taking that knowledge that you've built and doing something with it. If you have an idea, test it and see what happens.

Everything's an experiment until we put it out there, and I see business and life like that - it's just one big experiment. If I try something and it doesn't work out, that's great, I've learned something, but if I do it and it works, brilliant!

The same thing happened when I decided to do my 'Mastermind.' Initially, I was nervous, but I really wanted to do this to support women, so I decided to try and see what would happen. It was an amazing three-month experience, and we've had two further rounds since.

If you want to see growth in your business, you need to take action every single day and implement what you're learning.

Opportunity

The famous American author, Zig Ziglar made a quote that I heartily believe - *"success occurs when opportunity meets preparation."* This essentially means that you become successful when you're able to see opportunities and grab them with both hands. They are *everywhere*, but you have to be prepared.

You're not going to be able to do that if you're not clear on what it is that you want. For example, if you know that you want to interview a specific person for a podcast and then an opportunity presents itself to invite them onto your show, you can jump on it because you know that's what you want to do.

Being able to spot opportunities and being able to make quick decisions is key, and it goes back to being clear on what you want.

Remember - *"Success occurs when opportunity meets preparation"*

Action questions:
- In what area of your business do you need to practice more consistency?
- What things do you need to take action on that you are avoiding?

DESIGN TO WIN

This section is all about designing your dream business, having figured out what you want, what you're good at and what you enjoy.

One of the big challenges people face when going into entrepreneurship is making that shift from being an employee to being an entrepreneur. As an employee, you are hired to fulfil a function based on your particular skill-set, while someone else or another department may take care of admin, sales, marketing, etc. (unless that's the function you are in). The thing is, when you go into business, you now wear multiple hats. No longer are you just the coach, or the photographer, or the speaker, you're also the sales girl, the marketing chick, as well as the head of administration *and* customer care. It's a lot to take in.

Many people know how to fulfil their function, but not how to run a business, and unfortunately they complicate things for themselves.

To have a successful business you need to be able to solve a problem that people are willing to pay for and deliver that solution at a profit. Simple. Not necessarily easy, but definitely simple.

So the initial questions you want to ask yourself are:

1. **People** - *"Who do I want to work with? What kind of people do you want to help and why?"*

   We often find that we attract people very similar to ourselves, or where we were a few steps back. Where do they hang out? What are their biggest frustrations and challenges? How will you attract them into your community on a consistent basis?

2. **Problem** - *"what solutions do I bring to the market and is there a willingness AND an ability to pay?"* Some problems exist which, although they may be urgent, are not problem enough to motivate a person to part with their money. On the other hand, where the issue is pressing, and they need a solution NOW, people are willing to pay whatever is required to get it fixed. . You need to understand your market. It's not viable to want to provide a solution to a group of people who haven't got the means or the desire to buy it.to

3. **Packaging** - *"what am I offering?"* This is your product or service. When planning this out, think about the transformation you're bringing to your customer and what you need to provide in order

to help them experience that transformation. Don't start with the features (what is included) but rather the results.

Research your offer by speaking to people and assessing what else is out there in the market and how you can make yours better. Make sure that what you create is *relevant* to your ideal client and is delivered in the best way *for them.*

When creating your packages focus less on features, but on the transformation your client will get and, work backwards. What do they need from you and what do *they* need to do to achieve that result? These are things that people are concerned with.

4. **Positioning** -*"how will I market this offer and where do I want it to sit in the market. Am I high-end and low volume, or low-end and high volume?"* Thinking about the lifestyle that you want, where do you sit in the marketplace? How much hands-on action do you want your clients to get? How do you wish your brand to be perceived?

Within the online space, there are seven different business models you can use to create your own Full-time Freedom Business:

1. Freelancing
2. Coaching and Consulting
3. Information Products/e-learning
4. Software Development
5. Affiliate/Joint Venture partnerships
6. Subscription Membership Mode
7. Group Programs Model

Within services where I predominately operate, there are a further three options here;

1. Done for you
2. Done with you (teach me how to do it)
3. Self-study (I want to do it myself)

I started out as a freelancer offering website and graphic design services, then transitioned into information products and e-learning. I now provide coaching and consulting as well as a subscription membership model via The Collective (www.chichieruchalu.com/the-collective) I am also an affiliate for certain products too.

Only you know what works for you, which is based on your personal preferences. Revisit the first part of this section where I got you to define your vision and then choose the business model (you can choose more than one) which works for you.

GETTING STARTED: TIPS FOR SERVICE-BASED ENTREPRENEURS

When you are beginning your coaching/service-based business, there are some critical steps you need to go through first.

1. Your 'why' and the ultimate lifestyle you want to live; design your life first - how many hours do you want to work, what kind of clients, how many clients - and then build a business to support it. This is so important for keeping you motivated and making the right business decisions.

2. Your niche - who you work with, what kind of people they are and what industries. I work with female coaches, strategists and creatives, who are either in a 9-5 and want to go full-time, or have transitioned to a full-time business and want to scale up.

3. Your business model - go back to the first point. What kind of lifestyle do you want? Do you want a few 1:1 clients, or lots of clients in a group program? You decide. Do you want to have a course or a program? I wouldn't start with a course first as you need a decent size audience to make it viable, but it is not impossible.

4. Your USP (Unique Selling Point) - why you are different and how do you stand out. This is so important. In a sea of similar businesses, what sets you apart? Why should people choose you? Think about your story and why you're on this path, what are you passionate about, and what do you stand for.

5. Your customers and their problems - if you are a 'coach', remember that coaching is not a business but rather a skill that you use. What problems are you're solving for people?

For me, I help you get your business visible and grow it online. I am a digital marketer who uses coaching as a tool to reach my clients. What are your key skills that you will add your 'coaching' to? Don't forget any past knowledge or experience that you have. Often we come online and forget all our offline experience. I have over seven years experience working within the banking industry and with SMEs, as well as two years experience working for my local church which is also a charity.

6. Learn to talk about coaching (or your service-based business) in everyday language because the term "coaching" is used and interpreted differently by people.

Keep it simple - say who you help and how you can help them.

7. Create *one* specific package for a particular market (based on your unique expertise) and get really, really good at it. Build a solid client base, and *then* you can expand.

I focused on helping people with visibility and confidence, and now it's business growth as well. Once I nailed 1:1 coaching, I moved into group programs and masterminds. You can start with a group program if you wish. You decide.

Price your services accordingly based on the *results* you get people, not on hours worked. Think about the container in which you want to work with people. I originally started doing 90 days and found it wasn't long enough, so now I do 6-months coaching only and intensives for those people who want to deep, fast.

8. Work with someone who knows the industry and can help you fast-track your success – you don't have to spend years struggling to figure it out. Getting a mentor definitely moves you forward quicker, so you don't make

unnecessary mistakes. For me, even things like mapping out a client process, how to market and message myself, building my first funnels - a mentor helped with this.

9. Be visible consistently and offer up coaching/consult calls until you are fully booked. Again these can be market research sessions, actual free coaching or discounted intensives, where you charge say £99 for 2 hours and upsell people to a longer program afterwards.

The more calls you do, the more you hone your skills. Last year (2016) I spoke to over 70 women over the course of three months for free, which helped me gain insight into the way my ideal clients think, the real problems that they have and the best way for me to serve them. Be sure to gather up testimonials during this time too.

10. Create a lead magnet which speaks to your ideal client. A lead magnet is "an irresistible bribe offering a specific chunk of value to a prospect in exchange for their contact information. The goal of the Lead Magnet is to maximise the number of targeted leads you are getting for an offer.[1]"

---

[1]https://www.digitalmarketer.com/lead-magnet-ideas-funnel/

Other terms for this can be "freebie" or "opt-in", either way, the goal is the same - to get people to give you their email address or contact number so that you can ultimately sell them your offer.

For a coach or service based provider - the thank you page and email sequence is to lead them into a call with you - this is your lead generation and will be bringing people into your email list.

11. Communicate with your email list on a regular basis. Keep marketing your business, leveraging your social media platform of choice to make people aware of you, what you do and how you can help them.

12. Stay consistent.

DELEGATE TO DOMINATE

Crushing the Superwoman Syndrome

Do you feel that you have to be superwoman in your life? You can't ask for help, and you run yourself into the ground trying to do everything? Have you neglected self-care and are working all the hours with little rest or fun time? If the answer is yes, that's okay - this is a 'no-judgement' zone!

Some of us place ourselves right at the bottom of the priority tree. Neglecting the most important person in our businesses. If I asked you what you ate each day last week, would it be non-existent, junk food or healthy and nourishing?

I used to be this way, and if I am honest I have moments when I slip back into it, but ultimately I know that trying to be all things, to all people, leaves me tired and burnt out.

Today, I have no shame in asking for help in my life - whether it be with cooking, cleaning, housework or childcare. I believe that these things need to get done, but it doesn't have to be *me* who does them.

What things are draining you right now? What can you release, delegate or outsource? Whenever the word "outsource" is mentioned, people automatically think a Virtual Assistant or another support person, but what about delegating your:

* Grocery shopping to your local supermarket delivery service
* Social media posting to a tool like Smarter Queue or Buffer
* Sales activity (just some) to a quality website, (i.e. have a well-designed website, which can sell on your behalf 24/7)
* Diary management to an online scheduler to keep you organized. I like Acuity.

Delegating to dominate means thinking more strategically about how you are spending your time and having firm boundaries to ensure that you're getting the right stuff done every day. Don't have money to pay for things? Start small; there are a lot of free and low cost tools you can use. Check out the bonus hub to see my list of top tools to help you start and grow your business –
http://chichie.co/ifonlytheyknewbook.

Get clear from the start how many hours you have to dedicate to your business each week. Rather than pushing your business into your life, take your week and block off all the important things (including sleep) and see how much time you have left to run your business. Everyone has 168 hours in the week. Once you've blocked off those vital things, you will have a realistic number (of hours) and an idea of what you can give to your business.

I remember doing this exercise while I was in my 9-5 and realising I only had 8 hours a week to spend on my business. It doesn't sound a lot, but you can get a lot done when you focus on the important stuff, get help, and say no.

CEO DAY

At least once a month, take what I like to call a CEO day, where you spend time away from your business, working *on* your business. Take time to reflect on what's working well, what you need to stop and what you should continue doing. Plan your month, your quarter and get clear on your goals. So often we dive in, head first and spend so much time working IN our business that we don't have the time to reflect and work ON our business.

SELF CARE and why sleep is not overrated

A lot of you reading this book have to pay attention to more than just yourselves - a job, a demanding boss, a parent, a family, and business too. The importance of regularly filling your cup to be able to pour out to others cannot be overestimated. Self-care isn't always about spas and massages. For me, sometimes being able to read a book in peace, or have a nap interrupted can work wonders.

Check out my podcast episode from the CEO Mastery Podcast where I go deeper into this topic.

Listen here: http://chichie.co/ceo-mastery-podcast-009

Action questions:

* Write down your list of things that fill you up and ensure that you do at least of them every single week!
* Ask yourself - If you were fully supported in your business and life right now, what would that look like? Who would be helping you, what would you be doing?

SEASONS

Monday, August 28th, 2017; Facebook:

This evening I sat in the dark, rocking my three-year old to sleep. I carefully placed him in his bed and sneaked out of his bedroom, only to hear cries of "mummy come and lie with me." I had this feeling of deja vu.

I remember the nights when I would do this with my daughter and how frustrating it felt, wanting her to sleep, but she wouldn't sleep unless mummy was lying next to her. Inside of me I would cry with frustration, tiredness, and impatience. I had things to do....why wouldn't she let me do them?

Motherhood had been this enlightening and somewhat bewildering experience, learning new things and working hard to keep my mini human alive. Balancing the desire to do my own thing, rediscover my identity but also be there and present for her too.

I began my first business (virtual assistant) 9 months after she was born. The sleepless nights worked for me; I was always a bit of a night owl. I could work on my business, build my website, do client projects and nurse her back to sleep when she needed it.

To be honest, I don't remember sleeping properly for the first three years of her life, but then she started sleeping through the night, and it was as if those sleepless nights had never happened.

And then her brother came along. Fast forward three years and here I am again.

But this time I feel peace because I know "this time shall pass" and so I savour it. I breathe it in. I don't even take my phone into the room. While I sit in the dark, I just think and reflect.

Seasons....

Life passes by way too fast and it's easy to not enjoy the journey because you're wishing it away, hoping for the next phase of your life. But I have learnt, and am learning that my current situation is not my final destination. And I can choose to see it any way I like.

Going through a business lull? Not booking clients? Money not coming in?

It's a season.

Have a young family like I do means that you have less time to work on your business than someone who doesn't. Or maybe you have other commitments which require your time and energy and you wonder when it will ever end.

It's okay. This is only a season

What's your season telling you? What are the lessons you need to learn? How can you come to embrace and appreciate those lessons?

Your business will go through seasons. Your life will go through them. Know that "this too will pass".

SECTION 3:
RUNNING YOUR BUSINESS

BE INTENTIONAL

Don't do things just *because*.

Every action in your business should happen because you have decided it is going to happen. Having a "throw the spaghetti at the wall and see if it sticks" approach will leave you frustrated because you will never really know what works and what doesn't.

Don't look around at others and compare yourself and then feel bad. You are only seeing their highlights and have no idea what is going on behind the scenes. Set your own goals and milestones, and work towards achieving them.

Remember that this is your business. Yes, you can get strategies and tactics from others, but only you can determine what works in your business. For example, in the online space, a strategy that was promoted a lot for getting clients was spending time in Facebook groups. Now while this approach does work, it requires a lot of time investment.

I don't know your situation, but as someone who was running a business alongside a family and a job, this was not the best use of my time. Nor was it a strategy that would work well for me, so I had to figure out a plan that did. Read more on that later.

Get clear on your goals and track your results. I am a creative, but I also love spreadsheets and know the value of monitoring my numbers. It's easy to think that you are not on track with something, or that you are doing better than you are until you look at the numbers; numbers always speak the truth. I also track my social media numbers, email list, income, leads; you name it, it's tracked. Grab my tracking spreadsheet inside the bonus hub: **http://chichie.co/ifonlytheyknewbook.**

Remember, *"What gets measured gets improved"* - Robin S Sharma.

As I mentioned in an earlier chapter, you need to keep building your expertise and developing your skills. By doing so, not only will you be able to bring more value to your clients, you can charge more - your level of expertise is directly connected to the value that you bring to the marketplace.

When I started as a virtual assistant - just doing general work - I was charging £20-25 an hour and was no different to the next VA. As soon as I started to specialise and do more design and tech work, I realised I could charge more than £50/60 an hour because not many people could do design and my services were in demand. Continue to develop your skills and expertise.

Finally be intentional with your time. We all get the same amount of hours in the day, yet some people achieve so much more. What is your time worth and how are you leveraging it?

INVEST IN THE RIGHT TOOLS

I can't tell you the number of entrepreneurs I see trying to build their busy on ineffective tools. So, for example, let's look at client onboarding.

You can either do:
* Diary ping pong to book your appointment, wasting a lot of time
* Create a proposal in Word and send to your client
* Create a contract in Word, edit all the sections - every single time
* Send out said contract which your client needs to print, sign, scan and return

* Send an invoice in Word, which you create every time
* Once all signed and returned, send another Word document with a whole bunch of questions your client needs to answer as part of their intake form, which is so cumbersome because it's in Word.

OR

You can invest in a tool or tools that do it all for you, saving you an immense amount of time.

Benefits - Your client gets a smooth onboarding process, and your business looks as professional and efficient. To find out what tools I use, visit the book bonus hub:

http://chichie.co/ifonlytheyknewbook

I was in the first camp for a LONG time, and at one point I resented creating contracts and invoices because of how long it took, which meant that I didn't get paid as quickly as I could have or I lost opportunities because I was slow to respond back. Don't let that happen to you!

Another example is the kit you use. It took me ages to finally get my MacBook Pro because I kept trying to justify the expense. But the thing is, at some point, I realised that I was wasting so much time waiting for the old laptop to kick into action, that it was getting ridiculous.

I remember listening to a podcast by Chalene Johnson, and she said to invest in the best that you can afford because it is a false economy when you don't, which makes so much sense because I use my laptop every single day. I do everything in my business on it, so any time my laptop is not working, I am losing money. So it makes sense to invest in the best. When I got my new laptop - oh my goodness! - the difference it made to my productivity was incredible, and I have no regrets

CREATE THE RIGHT ENVIRONMENT

"You are the average of the five people that you spend your time with," according to Jim Rohn and equal to that, the physical environment from which you work in, also contributes to your level and quality of output in your business.

While we all love the laptop lifestyle and love the opportunity of working in yoga pants in our beds, there is a different feeling and attitude to work, when I sit down at my desk, in my home office or at a co-working space and get down to business.

Maybe it is just me, but my environment plays a huge role in how I feel and operate in my business. Now we all have to start somewhere, and for some of you, that might be the kitchen table, and that is okay too. Have a tray or box where you put all your work things so that it is easy for you to move them from location to location and then when you are working you have access to all the things you need to get your work done.

BUILD YOUR SYSTEMS

Having good systems will make running your business a whole lot easier. Whether it's a simple workflow for how you create your blogs posts or having a digital calendar so that you can stop the email ping pong and know how you are spending your time, you need always to be looking for ways in which to improve your business systems.

Key systems you need in your business:
* Email service provider
* Diary and appointment booking
* Taking payment

* Contracts and documents
* Communication

Download my recommendation for top tools in your business in the bonus hub:
http://chichie.co/ifonlytheyknewbook

Batching

Doing the same type of work together in one go can help with consistency and ultimately save you time because you are working in the zone, you have all the necessary tools set up already, and you can focus and get it done. Note - not everybody finds this technique helpful, so try it and see it for yourself. I like to batch content especially my podcast, social posts, and graphics.

Automation

This is using tools to make a workflow or a set of tasks happen automatically or without too much human intervention, once set up. Some tools are free, others require an investment.

Key areas to automate:
* Social Media, e.g., Buffer, Smarter Queue
* Client appointment booking, e.g. Acuity, Calendly
* Payment and Invoicing, e.g.Dubsado

* Email responses – use "canned" or templated responses

Outsourcing

What is the value of an hour of your time? I am not talking about what you charge out, but what is your time worth?

In an hour of my time, I can create a product that goes on to make me a £1000 for example. So to hire someone for £25 an hour to do a job makes sense.

Reclaim some of your time by outsourcing:
* Identify the tasks you want to outsource
* Start small and build up - I started with 5 hours/month.
* Document and improve your process as time goes on
* Think about time zone advantage - I regularly work with VAs in different time zones as they can be working while I am sleeping.

As Gina DeVee says *"You do not always have to be working on your business, but someone or something does"*.

If you're looking for more guidance when it comes to outsourcing and building your team, I go into more details about it, towards the end of the book.

Systemise

If you do it once and then do it again, create a system around it.

Why? There will be fewer mistakes, and you will have a minimum standard to which you operate. It is also easier to outsource because you have now created a workflow and you ultimately create a better client experience.

So how do you create a system? It can be as simple as a checklist or a video where you are doing the task and talking through the process. Whatever route you choose, the goal is to document what tasks you do in your business so that you can start to build a Standard Operating Procedure (SOP).

A SOP is simply a set of step-by-step instructions to help you (and your team) carry out routine activities in your business. SOPs help you achieve efficiency because the same steps are taken every time, so theoretically output and quality should be the same, regardless of who is doing the task and it also reduces miscommunication and ambiguity.

Some people think they need to wait until they have a team in place to start pulling together their SOPs - I disagree. Once you start doing similar tasks over and over, it's time to get them documented, and you will find it makes life easier when you bring people into your business having them already there.

Areas you can start to automate now:
* Client intake process
* Blog post creation
* Webinar set up
* Social media marketing
* Website admin

GET YOURSELF COVERED LEGALLY

The number of business owners I see working without simple things like contracts and client agreements is worrying. You need to have a client agreement or contract in place for all the work you do - this ensures that everyone is on the same page when it comes to the work being carried out and you are protected legally.

You can either get them prepared specially by a lawyer or attorney, or buy templates online which have been created by a lawyer. Be careful of doing a copy and paste job from what you see online as you might miss something and end up not be covered for what you need.

PLANNING TIPS

If it is not in my diary, it doesn't exist. I have both a digital diary and paper diary. Having a digital diary allows clients to book time into my diary with ease. I can see everything that is happening in my week at a glance and I can also time-block my day.

Sunday Night Planning
How do you get ready for the week ahead? This is how I plan (it's not always perfect but when I do it this way, the week is smooth):

First I sit down with my Google calendar, bullet journal, pens, and notepad, and I do a brain dump of everything in my head (#declutter).

I then review the diary for the week ahead to:
* Highlight any particular events for the week.
* Check for any birthdays so that I can send cards
* Determine my childcare requirements for the week, so that I can text my childminder and let her know

* Decide on what we're eating in the week, so I can pick up any missing things the next day when I head out to run errands

Finally, I list all the things I want to accomplish week for my business and in my house and assign them to different days of the week.

Monday is my admin and strategy day in my business. I follow up with things from the weekend, catch up with my team, follow up any leads and work *on* my business.

Tuesday is content creation/podcast recording.

Wednesday is content creation/client work and soon to be an additional coaching day.

Thursday is my coaching day.

Friday is review/wrap up and typically errands day.

On all those days, I fit in my *'Daily Five'* to ensure that I am doing something in my business every day to move it forward. The *Daily Five* are the five core activities you MUST do in your business every day to keep you visible, earning money and staying consistent and if that is all you do in a day, then you're good. More on this later.

I have learnt that when I plan, and I am organised, it makes life easier for me. It actually creates more freedom, ironically. Sure stuff comes up, and it's not perfect every week, but it gives me a baseline to work from.

How do you plan your week?

GETTING CLIENTS

I have run different types of businesses - from network marketing models to childminding, to being a Virtual Assistant, web and graphic designer and more recently coach and consultant, and every time I have had to go out and get clients.

If you're not booking clients consistently, it is usually down to one of five things:
1. You don't want them
2. You're not clear on who it is you want to attract
3. Your offer is not appealing enough
4. No one knows who you are
5. You are not asking for the sale

To access the full 'Get Clients Now' training go to :
http://chichie.co/ifonlytheyknewbook.

What were some of the things I did?

1. I got clear on the kind of clients I wanted to help, including their problems and how I could provide the solution. I looked to identify where they hung out and placed myself there
   You need to be crystal CLEAR on how you can help them and the results they will get.

2. I decided I wanted clients and looked to identify any fears I had about signing them up, which included child-care challenges and managing my diary around my job at the time.

3. I leveraged my network, i.e., told my friends and family what I did. In every business, my first clients were always friends or family. You will be surprised how many people don't know what you do. I email, text, post on my personal page what I do, so there is no mistake.

4. I got visible. As a childminder, I created my website long before it became a norm. I registered

my profile with a childcare site and the Local Authority's Family Information Services website and linked my website. I printed cards and left them everywhere. That was in 2012; if I were doing this today I would run Facebook ads, connect with local schools, etc.).

For my web and graphic design work I volunteered my services for free in my church and secured my first client that way. As a coach, I do live streams, blog, have a podcast and my **CEO Mastery**group.

5. I got organised. I got myself ready to receive clients. Whether that was my contracts or welcome packet - I got myself ready, because the last thing you want to be doing when someone says yes is to be scrambling around to get your stuff together.

6. I kept my eyes open for opportunities. There is work all around you if you are open to see it. Example of this; recently an old student of mine from my website course, mentioned in passing that she was thinking of updating her website as it was over two years old and it was no longer

responsive. I sent her a private message, we set up a call, and a couple of weeks later she had signed on as a web design client.

7. I do good work. Word of mouth is a great way to get repeat and new business. Look after your clients and they will keep coming back and also refer people to you.

As a coach, I see opportunities everywhere. I'm always listening and watching, and I'm not afraid to reach out and connect with someone (#sellingishelping).

What are ways that you can book new clients?

MY JOURNEY TO FULLY BOOKED

How would it feel to be fully booked in your business right now? Like, really - what would that mean to you?

For me, it meant security, consistency of income, peace of mind and freedom to work on new projects that I had been putting off for ages. *Plus* being able to leave my 9-5. At the time of writing this book, it's been a year since I left my "9-5 investor".

At the time, I had three 1:1 clients and 1.5 people in my new group program. I say 1.5 because she had said yes, but the funds hadn't yet hit my account. On September 22, I handed in my 30-day notice to my corporate job and set about filling my coaching practice.

I knew that because I loved community and didn't want to be hustling for discovery calls every month, I was going to leverage my time and enrol ten women into my new high-level group program. That would secure my income over the next six months.

I spent the next month on calls, live streaming, reaching out and following up and on 7th November when the program opened, I had filled ELEVEN spots, with a £22k launch.

What did that do for my business?
* My corporate income was replaced for the next six months
* My coaching practice was full with dreamy clients
* I had the headspace and freedom to create amazing new programs
* I could FINALLY launch my podcast and focus on other visibility activity

But most of all, what it taught me was that I could do anything I put my mind to. You see, I was someone who hated sales calls, and yet in the months before that launch I spoke to over 70 women for free, ran two challenges, did a live stream training every week and also just showed up and gave value to my community.

I believed in my program and challenged myself to be unselfish with my time. I made sure I showed up for myself and my program, to share with the world what I had to offer and allow the right women to come to me.

And so for those of you who are looking to get yourself booked out, know this:

* It can happen (if you want it to - **decide**)
* It starts with getting clear on what you want and why
* You **must** take daily action
* You have to **believe**
* It comes from a place of service

Now I know the system to book myself out, I know what works for me.

How many clients do you need to be officially booked out? How will you get your first or next clients?

CHOOSING FAITH OVER FEAR

Along your entrepreneurial journey, you are going to be faced with moments of fear on a regular basis.

Whether it's reaching out to your first client, or doing your first Facebook Live or maybe even pitching yourself for a guest publication, either way, fear is always going to come along for the ride. You are stretching yourself, doing new things and your mind is going *"Erm... what's going on, we don't like this"*, and so it will do whatever it can to protect and stop you from moving forward.

In every situation and opportunity, you will be presented with two choices. Faith or Fear.

And both of them cannot operate at the same time.

There have been times when I have just had to take a leap of faith. I've known the bigger goal and the bigger vision, but I didn't know how to get there, and I only could see the next step in front of me.

Sometimes, I'm simply going through a dry spell, I'm struggling and really want to give up but know deep down that quitting is not my path. It is in those moments where you question yourself, and you have to choose faith. I have had to step out and trust God.

You are the keeper of your dream. No one else.

Am I saying it will always work out? No, not always.

But I'm always glad I took the step anyway. I have too many personal experiences to know that life is short. Tomorrow is not guaranteed, so we need to embrace and maximise today. And when I've taken that leap of faith and things have worked out right, it's been amazing.

So, what is it going to be?

False Evidence Appearing Real or Face Everything And Rise?

Keep taking action.

STAYING THE COURSE WHEN YOU FEEL LIKE QUITTING

Running a business is hard work, but it's also deeply rewarding.

When you take an idea and bring it to life and have people give you money for it… that feeling? It's something else!

It will probably be one of the hardest ventures you ever have to do because you will be creating something from a vision that only you can see, and your well-meaning friends and family just won't get it. In fact, they will encourage you to quit, get a job, do something else but deep down you know you would never do that because this is your soul's calling.

Some days you will just want to walk away from it all - Like it is just too hard. Money isn't coming in. Bills need to be paid. It feels too *hard*!

I've been there.

You might even start looking at jobs again because surely that would be easier, right? Wrong. It's not. Remember it's having to work for someone else, on their schedule, with their rules. Easier? I don't think so.

But let me assure you...feeling this way, it's okay. It's normal.

YOU ARE NOT A FAILURE

This is a season, and it will pass if you don't quit. I'm not going to sugar-coat it - you will get tested repeatedly. Your resolve will be tested, but my question to you is *just how badly do you want it?* Don't allow your current reality to consume you, but instead focus on what you want to create in your life.

Focus on the things you can be grateful for today. Focus on the destination and embrace the journey. It's less about reaching the destination, and more about enjoying the person you are becoming on your way to getting there.

Stay in the room. Stay the course. Hold on until you succeed, because *this too shall pass.*
"The only failure is quitting, everything else is just gathering information" - Jen Sincero.

Love this quote, because it is so true. I've made a ton of mistakes along my entrepreneurial journey, and at times I have felt really bad, but the truth is that those errors only made me better and stronger. If you knew the sacrifices and regular "gathering of information" I go through, you would probably cringe. I sometimes do, and they are my mistakes!.

How do *you* see failure?Is it your opportunity to quit? Or your chance to push forward, gather the lessons learned, apply them and move forward?

Entrepreneurship is not for everyone. But it is 100% worth it.

You never lose. You either win, or you learn. I have had moments when I have made some poor decisions, and I would be lying if I said I didn't want to bury myself inside a cave and never come out at those times.

Earlier this year I tried to build a design agency. And I say "tried" because while it was something I wanted to do, and I found the most amazing team members, it was the wrong time, the wrong model, the wrong everything. Trying to grow two baby businesses at the same time was hard.

I felt conflicted as to where I should spend my time. And trying to scale a business that I had successfully run solo was even harder. I wasn't 100% sure on the offerings I wanted to lead with and be known for, and so I spent a lot of time figuring it all out. My focus and energy were split, and it ended up impacting my coaching business more than I realised because I took my eye off the ball especially when it came to costs and numbers.

I quickly realised that to be profitable, I needed to completely shift the target market I was operating in, and I wasn't ready to operate at that level. I lost money because I didn't price our projects appropriately and once I had paid my team, I was left with very little.

The most significant realisation I had was that while I loved working on creative projects, I didn't want to run a big team. In my ideal work scenario, I prefer to liaise with one person, and THAT person manages the team. I found it stressful having to project manage, coordinate, market, sell AND run the coaching business. I know my strengths, and the whole experience taught me A LOT of lessons, which is why I always take you back to *"What is the lifestyle you want? What is your vision? What is your genius power?"*

Making mistakes is the norm as an entrepreneur, we are required to "fail fast" so we can learn and move on. How quickly you pick yourself up and keep moving forward will determine how far you go.

"KAIZEN" - THE ART OF CONTINUOUS IMPROVEMENT

As a natural troubleshooter, I am always looking for ways to improve and make things better. When I learnt Six Sigma back in my Project Management days, I learnt about the concept of Kaizen - a Japanese business philosophy of continuous improvement of working practices, personal efficiency, etc[2].

Sometimes as entrepreneurs, it is really easy to do something once, decide it was okay and then move onto something else, rather than refine and make it better.

Obviously, if something flops badly, don't try and resurrect it, but say you release a new program or course and 3-5 people sign up. That is not a failure. It just means that you didn't get yourself in front of enough people to market yourself. Do it again, with more visibility; you will get more numbers. The fact that you sold three means that people are interested.

The very first Mastermind I ran in January 2016 - *Purpose, Passion and Profits Mastermind* - I had six women in the program. I was scared - this was my first group program - and so I wrote a list of the women I wanted to have in the group, and I invited them. I didn't even promote it outside of that or tell my email list.

It was a small intimate group, and I learnt a lot about running a group program and making sure it fit around

---

[2] www.dictionary.com

my lifestyle, rather than the other way round. I remember doing group calls, with my then one-year-old baby on my back, video off, jumping him up and down to sleep. It was then I decided I no longer would do calls in the evening.

At the end of the three months, we had an in-person day which was magical, and I learnt that there is something super powerful when women connect face to face. Tears flowed and lifelong friendships made.

My second Mastermind was the *Visibility Vortex Mastermind* in Nov 2016, which focused on helping you grow in confidence and upping your visibility. I took the lessons from the first Mastermind, increased the number of spaces and included 1:1 calls. I hosted the group coaching calls in the day and had 11 women sign up. My goal was 10.

This was the program that supported me in the first six months of going full-time and replaced my corporate income. I worked my butt off for the preceding month and a half doing calls, connecting with people and inviting people into the program, and it was filled!

A few things I didn't factor was:

* Different business types: product vs. service
* Different stages of business owners: just starting vs. more experienced, different needs
* The importance of a group being able to bond well from the get-go (very important!)
* Having different levels of access to me, so if you wanted 1:1 you could upgrade (I offered it to everyone)

The 1:1 calls were fantastic, but the Facebook group? Tumbleweed. I tried several times to resurrect it but in the end recognised that if you don't set the intention clearly at the beginning and have the members of the group also agree to this, it is difficult to get it later. Huge lesson there.

I also asked the ladies who were part of the program for their feedback and listened to what they said. They gave me nuggets I could use for future programs.

I was so discouraged by the lack of group engagement I almost wrote the program off. I had almost decided "never again!" but my mentor asked me to clarify whether that was necessary or whether I could look at ways to make it better the next time. I chose the second option (because I genuinely love group programs), learnt lessons from this program and allowed it to influence my next Mastermind - The Inner Circle 1.0.

Ahhh, the Inner Circle (Now Elite). This has been my best group program to date.

I took the feedback, my observations and the things that I had learnt and created a new program, which focused on community and strategy for women in years 1 to 3 of business, earning less than £2000 a month.

This group was focused on giving women a safe space to grow, learn and share. There were Accountability Pods to support in-between group calls, Pop-up Challenges, Mini Trainings and coaching from me.

I gave all the ladies a questionnaire to complete at the beginning of the program so that I could understand their needs and motivations and I also used this information to pair them into their accountability pods.

The women gelled from day one *and* showed up. I was very intentional about this and set the tone from the beginning of what I expected of them.

Throughout the program, I didn't have to worry about people not coming into the group, posting or asking questions. The ladies stepped up and supported each other and I was able to be a mentor, coach, and facilitator. I loved being able to deliver this program, and as my clients grew in confidence, there were shifts in mindset, new businesses started, measurable growth in fledgling businesses, and more.

One of my clients made more money in the first month of the program than she had ever made, her entire time in business!

I also learned that it is important to listen to feedback and evolve. To "vet" people beforehand to ensure that they are a right fit.

I handpicked all the accountability groups and they worked well. I also made sure that I led by example and showed up each day. If I made a mistake, I didn't hide it and when part way through they said they wanted more coaching calls (not part of the original package), I obliged because their results were important to me.

Always keep listening and developing.

When something you have is good, but some part of it is not working, learn to evolve. Shift and change. If I hadn't done that with Vortex Mastermind, the Inner Circle would not have been born and neither would **The Collective**.

Be sure to bring KAIZEN into your business and look to improve - every single day.

SOWING SEEDS

Many times, I get people telling me how they get discouraged that they're out there marketing their business, posting on social media and hearing crickets and wondering whether they should stop.

If you are feeling the same, here is one thing I want you to understand.

Think of marketing like a farmer sowing seeds. He knows that one day he will receive a harvest of his crop, but before that time, he has to remain consistent with watering and nurturing his fields - building upon the actions of the day before. He knows his seed is in the ground and he is watching and nurturing it until Harvest day comes for our farmer and he sees a bountiful supply.

Back to marketing. A lot of you don't realise that people are watching you. They may not be commenting and liking, but they are watching. If you're just getting started with posting on your Facebook page or Instagram, or you are beginning to re-engage and no one is commenting, it doesn't mean that you are not doing a good job, or that your content is rubbish.

No feedback doesn't mean stop.

In fact, you should carry on, because business is all about consistency. You are building leverage and digital assets. You are also building good habits.

How many things do you see or watch on social media that you don't like or leave a comment for? Me? Loads.

Last year I committed to being visible every single day and it paid off.

Marketing has a 90-day window, so whatever you may be doing today, you will see the true results in around three months.

Lessons:
* Remain consistent.

* Keep sowing good seeds - quality content, building relationships
* Continue to show up and build trust with your audience.
* Don't be discouraged.

PUSHING OR PULLING?

Recently I had a client session where we were discussing how she could increase her visibility and attract new clients into her business.

She didn't want to be pushy, all over the place or in people's faces in an aggressive way, but be able to showcase her expertise and demonstrate how she could help them in a way that felt good.

I shared with her the concept of 'push and pull marketing,' both of which are very different and describe the method with which you approach your prospective clients.

PUSH marketing is more aggressive and is where you take your product or service to the consumer.

PULL marketing is where you do your thing (being brilliant at what you do and who you are) and allow your ideal clients to be drawn into you.

So what might this look like in the online space?

PUSH marketing
* Spamming Facebook groups and social media with messages all about your products and services adding NO value
* Creating products and services no one wants by ignoring what they want and need and being determined to sell it no matter what
* Speaking at (instead of with) prospects and customers
* Sending out messages to unwilling, unreceptive people via Messenger or email
* Friending someone on Facebook and then immediately messaging them to join your group or even worse *adding* them to your group (my biggest pet peeve for sure)
* Bombarding your email list with constant offers and no value

PULL marketing

* Taking the time to listen to your ideal client whether it is through social media, interviews or email
* Storytelling and humanising your brand through vulnerability and authenticity
* Creating content that engages your target audience and sharing it
* Creating amazing user experiences that leave a lasting impression and have them craving for more
* Delivering fantastic customer service that "wows"
* Having a website which can provide potential clients all the info they need to make a buying decision 24/7
* Being strategic in your emails, sending value and building the relationships

Through the power of PULL marketing you don't have to be out there doing what everyone else is doing, with the 24/7 hustle. NO. You be you.

You get clear on who you want to attract, get clear on your message, listen to what your people are saying and give them solutions to their problems. By doing so, you don't have to compete on price. Your ideal clients will want to work with you *and* they will come looking for you.

An example of an excellent brand which uses PULL marketing very well is Apple. Think about what they do to engage their followers. They create stories around the brand and products. They create huge anticipation around their products, and by the time those products are released, people are begging Apple to take their money.

MY PERSONAL STRATEGY - LIGHTHOUSE

I want to shine so brightly that people are drawn to me.

I focus on delivering amazing high-value content via my blog, podcast and live streams either on my platform or the platform of others.

From there people are intrigued and are drawn into my community, CEO Mastery (www.ceomasterygroup.com). I then continue to nurture the relationship and ultimately convert people into customers.

I decided that I didn't want to hang out in Facebook groups (except initial research purposes), but instead, I wanted to build a community and establish myself as the leader, expert, and authority.

This strategy works for me, and I encourage my clients to do the same because we all would rather buy from a leader, not a follower.

BE VS DO - WHAT GOT YOU HERE ISN'T GOING TO GET YOU THERE

The mindset, systems, and strategy that you had to get started need in and up-leveled.

As you learn and experience more, you can bring more to the table. You can be more. And your clients get to witness and experience this.

When I first started coaching, the thought of charging £5000 for a six-month package seemed foreign to me. Like *"No way! Who would pay that much?"*

It wasn't until I paid that much myself (more in fact) that I started to become comfortable to sell at that level. But I had to work on my mindset big time. I had the package on my website for MONTHS before anyone bought it. I went back and forth adjusting the price until in the end, I just put it out there and left it.

I had to work on my own self-belief and self-worth. Those stories that I was telling myself that I was an imposter or not good enough...I had to let them go.

I flipped it around to become *"what kind of woman do I need to be?"* for me to offer £5000 packages that people sign up for and don't bat an eyelid.

I worked on myself. I worked on my business. I got to a place where it became my 'new normal'.

When I sold my first package at that price, something shifted in me. And I've gone on to sell many more at that level.

'FUTURE YOU' DECISIONS

Make Decisions Based On Where You Want To Be, Not Your Current Reality.

What stories do you need to stop telling yourself so that you can confidently charge what you want and attract the clients you desire?

What kind of person do you need to become to achieve the results you crave?

Life is a mirror, and so if I find myself attracting people or things that are not what I want, I always ask myself in which areas of my life am I displaying those negative behaviours and what I need to change. It is a very insightful exercise.

"Success is not something you attain, it is something you attract by the person you become"- Jim Rohn.

NOT SETTLING

Since I was 18 years old, I have always wanted an Apple Mac.

A total tech nerd, I spent my summer holidays working alongside my dad at his design and print company. He taught me how to create newsletters and flyers using desktop publishing software, and I got to play with computers all day (did I tell you I was a nerd?).

I remember all my dad's computers were Apple Macs - the beautiful coloured ones that they used to have back then, and I loved them.

"When I get older I will get one," I said.

The time came to a head off to university, and I needed a new computer. Walking through PC World, I came across the MacBook, fell in love, looked at the price tag and my heart sank.

I walked out with a Toshiba laptop, which ended up being the worst computer I have ever had in my life. Always crashing, slow, the blue screen of death...aargh! Windows, why?!!!

Anyway, I still didn't have my Mac.

Fast forward ten years and my father-in-law had gifted me a Gateway laptop. Hey, it did the job, and I wasn't complaining. And then it died. Slap bang in the middle of maternity leave, funds were low, and so it was by pure miracle that one of my friends from church forwarded me a link to Dell where they had a crazy deal on entry level laptops.

For £162 I bought myself a replacement. And again it did the job.

And that's what I used as my business grew.

I have built websites, created graphics, done webinars and more on this Dell laptop than I could have imagined, which to be honest, surprised me. And so when the trackpad went, and I found myself spending more time waiting for it to do stuff than actually doing stuff, I knew it was time (see section on "Investing In The Right Tools") So on my vision board the MacBook Pro went.

Deep down inside I decided that I was not going to settle again.
Everyone I had spoken to who owned a Mac only sang its praises for what a solid machine it was and how long it lasted. And that sold it for me.

Anyway, this is not an ode to Apple. It is about not settling.

In life and business, we will be presented with opportunities to do or get things for ourselves. For whatever reason, some of you will tell yourselves that you don't deserve this, and you will either sabotage yourself or choose something inferior rather than what you want.

And the thing is, not settling doesn't always mean going for the most expensive option, this is about choices and choosing what it is *you* want.

So for example, maybe you know you want to work with a particular coach and rather than ask yourself *"How can I afford this? What can I do to find the money?"*, you settle for a cheaper coach who doesn't give you want you need, and you don't 100% enjoy the experience.

Or maybe, rather than investing in the singing all-in-one software, you would choose to make do with lots of separate subscriptions to things which end up costing more time and money because they don't talk to each other.

It could be jobs, relationships, locations... whatever. The point is that you're settling if you choose something that isn't truly what you want.

Identify what it is you want, and decide within yourself that you will go for *that*. No matter what.

Because life is meant for living and we attract more of the same into our lives, so settle in one area you will settle everywhere. I want you to stop settling. Like right now, stop. Don't do it.

You deserve more.

Oh and that MacBook? I am writing from it right now!

INVESTING IN YOURSELF

A lot of people think they can build their business on "free". Free information, free cheat sheets, free challenges. Free! Free! Free!
And sure you can get knowledge, but it will only take you so far.

You are not even prepared to put your hand in your pocket and invest even an hour with a mentor or coach you *know* will help move your business forward. Or join an affordable program or membership site.

Know this: in order to grow you have to invest yourself. You can't cut corners and do things on the cheap - business success does not work that way.

Investing in your personal development will pay far bigger dividends than any other investment and you *cannot* expect anyone to invest in you if you don't invest in yourself.

Over the past five years I have spent close to £50k on training, coaching, mentoring and programs and I have no shame in admitting this.

Throughout my business journey, there has been one thing that has really helped push my business forward A LOT - Taking leaps before I was ready to take them.

Whether it was hiring my first VA.
Purchasing a course I knew would help my business.
Investing in a business coach.

Launching or closing a service.

I had to take the leap and jump.

In all of these situations, did I feel ready? Heck no! Some of the times I didn't even have the funds. But I knew what I needed to move me forward and take me closer to achieving my goal of leaving my 9-5 and doing this full-time. Why?

Because I believe in the power of investing. I constantly 'uplevel' myself so that I can be the best.

I also know the principle of sowing and reaping and every time I have invested into myself or my business, I have made it back. Many times over.

Did I always have the money?

No, but I took advantage of payment plans and other avenues. Now I am not saying that you get into debt, but there are ways you can invest in yourself and leverage the investment. Sometime family can help, other times you create an offer and sell it, which helps fund your first payment. Always be mindful of investing in the right thing for you, at the right time.

One thing I do know, if you don't invest in yourself, I can guarantee a year from now you will still be in the same place. Moaning. Complaining. Disappointed. Frustrated.

Still doing FREE.

Decide on what you need right now in your business (just in time learning) and get support for that.

Complete the course, coaching program or training. Implement what you know and get an ROI, then move forward.

What investments do you need to make today?

MEASURING GROWTH - THE THREE CS

For me, the way I measure growth in my business is to look at three core areas.

Clients - how many do I have right now? How many new clients have I signed, whether it is for low cost or higher value offers? If I am not increasing my client base, then I am not growing.

Community - this includes my email list and my Facebook Group, CEO Mastery (www.ceomasterygroup.com). If they are growing, then I know that my reach and impact are growing too.

Cash - income into my business. Pretty straightforward.

Remember, we always seek progress over perfection and when starting out, your goals in this area might be:
- get your first client
- 100 people on your email list
- make your first £1000

Stay in your lane. Overwhelm comes from comparing yourself to others, losing your focus and not knowing what your own goals are. You can avoid and minimise overwhelm by staying on track with what you want to do.

FEELING LONELY

The stuff no one talks about.

Feeling alone in your business? Business *is* lonely, but only if you make it so.

Yes, you have the freedom and the autonomy butessentially it is you and your laptop when you're working online, which is why community is so important.

Don't be an island. Connect with others.

Get a biz bestie, join a mastermind.
Grab a real coffee or a virtual one.

Network and go to events.

Be intentional about surrounding yourself with other high vibe women.

Feeling lonely? Do something about it.

NO WOMAN IS AN ISLAND

True visibility starts with being visible with yourself.
Tuesday, September 19th 2017; Facebook:

Authenticity always wins, but yet we are afraid to let down the mask.

What will people think, say or feel about me?
I can't bear it if people no longer like me, or judge me
What if people discover who I really am and realise that I am not all that... I am not that put together.
They will be hugely disappointed.

The deep desire for acceptance and approval is HUGE and at the same time can be the BIGGEST PRISON you can put yourself IN.

I know this personally.

Trapped in this space of approval and acceptance from others, when in fact I already had it - if I chose to open my eyes and see it.

Acceptance from God.
Acceptance and approval from myself.

WHAT WOULD YOU DO TODAY IF YOU DIDN'T CARE WHAT OTHERS WOULD THINK OF YOU?

What message would you bring to the world if you fully believed in yourself and didn't chase the likes and accolades, but simply shared from the heart?

Will you choose authenticity over popularity or become one of the crowd, blending it, trying to be like others, rather than standing for what you believe even if it means standing alone?

So today as I write this, I want to reflect on the reality of being an entrepreneur and how most days it is really hard.

That sometimes the pressure of having a "following" means that you are too scared to do what you actually want to do, for fear of letting people down or what people will think.
And the more people that follow you and come into your community, the more you retreat and freak out a little more.

That the Instagram highlight of glossy pictures and big smiles doesn't show the insecurities, piles of dirty laundry, tantrums and daily life of as a wife and mum who is just trying to keep it all together raising her kids as best as she can.

That you constantly have people all around you who are doing MILES better (in your opinion) and therefore trigger the hell out of you, whenever they appear on your news feed and then distract you from doing what YOU should be doing.

That I've spent more time looking at job adverts in the last 3 months, wondering 'what if?'.

But it's all good, it is well.

Because this is life. Real life.

In my devotion this morning (which full transparency here has been totally neglected the past few weeks), Joyce Meyer mentioned that whatever we focus on we become.

So today I choose to focus on living an authentic and real life.

Focus on gratitude and grace. Forgiveness and faith.

It's messy but it's real.

It's me.

It's not everything I do that you will like.
Nor everything I say you will resonate with, but that is okay.

True visibility starts with being visible with myself, honouring myself and that is what is important, for you and for me.

Everything you need is inside of you.

WEEKDAY WARRIORS - FOR ALL MY 9-5 HUSTLERS

WHY GETTING A JOB WILL ACTUALLY SAVE YOUR BUSINESS, NOT KILL IT

Hustle. Quit. Take the leap. Leave.

These are all the messages we are bombarded with when we are part-time entrepreneurs, building our businesses alongside a job. The notion being that to be successful you have to be all in, or you're not fully committed.

As a Business Coach and Strategist who works with a lot of women who have jobs and families, I say this is complete nonsense. I don't believe you need to leave your job to have a successful business, nor sacrifice your life to get there. One of my mastermind friends, Holly MacCue has built a six figure business working 3 days a week in her high powered corporate job and 2 days in her business, so it is definitely possible.

In fact, if anything, I believe people leave their jobs too soon, putting an enormous amount of pressure on themselves. They have no real plan and struggle for money, lose focus, the business flops, and they end up going back to a job.

Two and a half years ago I was in a similar place. An established web designer coming towards the end of my maternity leave, I decided to change direction and focus more on Business Strategy. My existing business model was no longer sustainable, I wasn't earning enough, and I had no choice but to go back to a job.

Was I disappointed? For sure. In fact, I felt like I was going backwards and that I had failed, but then I had a massive reframe.

I can honestly say that going back to work saved my business and here are five reasons why:

1 - Clarity of your purpose

Working a job alongside your business will do one of two things: either reaffirm that you are on the right path as an entrepreneur or confirm that actually, this is not really for you.

For me, it was the former. I realised that while my job served a purpose, it was not my purpose and it fuelled a daily fire within me to do whatever I needed to do, to make my business succeed. Sitting at my desk at work, I realised how much I missed my regular client interaction, doing fun things with my children and being in full control of my days.

Added to that, you know how they say that *"the grass is always greener"*? Well it helped me to fully appreciate the freedom I had working for myself, and I was determined to get that back.

2 - Realignment of Priorities and Laser Focus

Go back to work - even if it is just part time - and you're now dedicating approximately 25 - 45 hours per week to help grow someone else's business. Once I got over that realisation, I quickly realised that any time available to work on my own projects was not to be wasted. Factor in two young children and focus and productivity became a priority.

Are you really going to mess around and waste the time you have? Not really. You get focused on your income generating tasks. You become resolute on being visible, and you do the work. Consistently.

Why? Because that is what you need to do and you haven't got time to waste. You get clear on your goals and take action on them. Every single day.

Side note - if you find yourself wasting time, then that is something more profound and most likely a form of self-sabotage (whole other topic).

3 - Financial stability

No one likes to worry about money at the best of times. But living on your savings while you build your empire can be a burden and a distraction. And that is if you even have savings to dip into. Most people don't!

If you jumped before you were ready, then you will find yourself focusing solely on the money. Under pressure to cover your essentials, you start to operate from a place of desperation, taking on clients you would typically say no to and repelling the ones you should actually be working with.

Why would you want that?

I like the fact that I can say no to projects which are not the right fit.

A job brings the stability of regular income so at the very least you know your essentials are covered. You can make investments in your business if and when you need to (and you will need to).

Money worries are like this big black cloud that follows you everywhere you go. It is a huge creativity killer, and it distracts you from the real work you should be doing.

Allow your business to start earning the income you want, on a consistent basis.

4 - Better support for my business and personal life

"If you're overwhelmed with too much on your plate, it's because you don't have enough support." - Marulabichela

The first few six months of going back to work were tough. I'm not going to lie. Trying to juggle a busy corporate position, children, and my business... I did not have the right support in place on all fronts in order to thrive.

I quickly realised that the most successful women in business are those who learn to delegate. They know their strengths and know their limits. Anything they are not able to do, they pass on. Guilt-free.

For me, relinquishing control, building a team and trusting others was a learning curve, but now I wouldn't have it any other way. I am fully supported in my business and my life, and this has allowed me to be on the front foot and grow my business from a place of ease.
Remember, you are a leader. Delegate and dominate.

5 - Improved business model and income diversification

Have you heard the statistic that most millionaires have 5-7 income streams?

I had the mindset that I work for myself, and that my job was my biggest client and one of my many income sources.

While the 1:1 model is the fastest way to bring cash into your business, it is not sustainable. If you get sick, or you can't work there's no income.

So I knew that I needed to find ways to leverage my time. One of the reasons I transitioned away from my web design business was that it was not a scaleable business model. It required me to be *in* my business all the time, and that was not the life I wanted to create for myself.

The birth of my son and subsequently returning to work forced me to think outside of the box -How else could I earn money in my business if I removed the 1:1 model?

I started to explore other business models including group work, courses, workshops and digital products and now I earn money from many different sources.

Would I have eventually introduced all of these things if I was working solely in my business? Yes, most likely, but I accelerated the implementation of it all because the benefits had an immediate impact.

I also got smart and used technology to automate, delegate and systemise as much as I could.

You're probably asking *"so when is the right time to make the leap?"*

Only you can answer that, but know this - you want to be doing it at a stage where your business has a model that is working and is bringing in consistent income.

Be open to the lessons you are learning while being in your job and see how you can transfer this to your business. Realise that Rome was not built in a day and no sustainable business is built overnight.

Create your escape plan and do it correctly. The last thing you want is to leave your job, only to have to go back.

Ain't nobody got time for that!

MAKING THE LEAP

At the time of writing this book, it has been one year since I resigned from my corporate job. I knew for a long time that I wanted to get out. I didn't really want to go to a job, but at the time, it was the right decision for our family. In May 2015 I set myself a goal of twelve months and then I would be out.

Twelve months went by, and I was still in my job, and I freaked out a little. What the heck was happening, why had I not left yet, why I had not achieved this goal?

At the time my initial plan was to pay off all my debt first, then leave, but that soon became apparent that if I took that approach, I would still be working for someone else for a few years yet. So I made peace with the fact that my debts were still going to be in existence as a full-time entrepreneur and looked to pursue other options.

I then decided that if I was going to leave, I had to have certain things in place My goal was to secure six months worth of income, essentially replacing my corporate income.

Was I scared? Sure I was! But I also knew that I had reached a point in my business where it was a real struggle to do any more. There were no more hours in the day and no more capacity and so I had to make a decision.

I remember deciding that I was going to hand in my notice in October; I asked God for a clear sign that it was the right next step and got it the very next day when I received a call from my manager asking me if I had a side hustle.

As the call developed, I realised that this was my sign to make a decision about my business and job and take the leap. I ended the call giving my 4-week notice and left three weeks later with a week's holiday.

You can watch my video of my last day at http://www.chichieruchalu.com/last-day-9-5/.

Only you will know when the time is right to leave. You may never feel 100% ready - you'll simply have to trust and jump.

SECTION FOUR:
THE CONSISTENCY QUADRANT

STAYING CONSISTENT

Want to know the one thing that stands between you and the success you desire in business?

Consistency.

Staying the course. Every single day.

Consistency is about having that belief and trust. It is about showing up, even when no one is watching and doing what you said you were going to do. When I decided to become consistent with my visibility, I would upload my videos pretty much every day and, to be honest, I wasn't getting any comments. Nobody was showing up. When Facebook Live first came out I'd go live, and nobody would come and watch, but I knew I needed to keep doing it and as a result, I grew in confidence. I was getting more comfortable, and that's what consistency brings.

So many of us struggle with being consistent in business, even in the simplest of tasks and for me, the biggest frustration with that is you are always stopping and starting, losing momentum.

There are four areas in business that I feel every entrepreneur needs to have consistency in, to grow and have a successful and strong foundation. They include:

* **Mindset and Confidence**. What you believe to be true about who you are and what you can accomplish.

* **Visibility and Community.** You need consistency in your visibility and in growing your community and your email list.

* **Strategy and Systems.** You need to have a strategy and be consistent in actually executing that strategy. Not just doing it one day, then forgetting about it the next day and moving on to something new only to decide that's not working either. It's about having a really good, strong strategy and implementing it every day.

* **Money Mastery and Sales.** If you're somebody who hasn't got a great relationship with money, this pours out into your business too and you may find that you struggle with making consistent income.

On my journey to leaving my job, I had to spend dedicated time to get to grips with my finances and my business finances in particular, as I knew it was the final step that was holding me back from taking the leap.

I was one of those entrepreneurs who could never really tell how much money I was earning. Then when it came to doing my taxes - oh my goodness - it was this painful experience of going through all my different accounts, PayPal and Stripe, trying to bring it all together.

It got to a point where I realised I couldn't continue to do this if I want to have a business that was going to be successful financially. So, I spent the time and got to grips with my numbers. I got to grips with everything going in and out, and that was a great exercise actually, for really culling things that were not necessary.

So in reviewing those four areas, ask yourself, *"where am I struggling?"*

Mindset and Confidence
Visibility and Community
Strategy and Systems
Money Mastery and Sales

Last year (2016) my area of weakness was my visibility and systems. I knew I was good at what I did but no one knew about me, so I decided to become consistent with showing up every day, even though it felt like I was on my own for most of it.

The result? Record business growth and being able to finally walk away from my 9-5.

I want to share with you five reasons why you are currently not consistent in your business and what you can do about it.

1. You aren't clear on your vision

You are not clear on what it is that you're trying to achieve and because of that you haven't set any clear goals. It's like going on a journey without a destination in mind.

When you don't have a clear vision, you will find yourself doing things that are not getting you any closer to your goals.

Your vision is intrinsically linked to your "why" and therefore when things get tough and challenging, you will just give up. Ask yourself, *"What do I want? What is my big vision for my life and business? How will this particular activity contribute to the overall accomplishment of that vision?"*

2. You're setting yourself up for failure

First, identify the things that can sabotage your success. Human nature means we always go for the path of least resistance. When left to make a decision in the heat of the moment, we cave.

Planning can help you stay on the consistency train.

For example, if you are struggling with publishing blog content on a regular basis, schedule ongoing brainstorming sessions to map it all out. Set yourself up for success.

Often, we have activities and tasks that we know we need to do, but we don't spend the time to figure out how to make life easier for ourselves. In fact, we sabotage ourselves because we don't plan for success. Think about what you're trying to achieve and prepare for it.

3. You're not 'eating that frog'

I like to batch things on certain days. I like to do client calls on a certain day, content creation on another day, etc. I also like to do things very early in the morning so I know it's done and I can enjoy my day. I even schedule in my Facebook Live videos. Why? Because if I don't, it doesn't happen.

By identifying essential tasks and scheduling them I am doing what Brian Tracy calls "eating that frog" (i.e., doing my most challenging task first). Then I know that it's done and out of the way.

What is it that you need to do? Take your big vision and break it down into goals (e.g., annual, monthly, and daily). Next, plan it — write it down — on your schedule. Once it's in your planner it's non-negotiable — get it done.

4. You're making excuses

You decide there is a better reason why you shouldn't do it. This type of excuse is often rooted in fear or other self-limiting beliefs.

Think about something you haven't been doing on a regular basis. What is holding you back?

Often, the first response is, "I haven't got time."

Actually, we always have time to do the things we really want to do. Instead, dig deep to understand what the real excuse is and the underlying fear associated with it? By taking a close look at your excuses and the ways you self-sabotage, you become more aware.

Outside of that, many excuses are cloaked in laziness. You don't want to do the hard work involved to get the result you say you want.

5. You don't have public accountability

When you connect with other people, tell them, *"This is what I want to do. Hold me accountable."* It works and it helps you get stuff done.

Public accountability can be the catalyst you need to keep moving. Personally, knowing that I have to report back to my Mastermind on tasks I said I would do keeps me from slacking off!

Even if you do something as simple as creating a calendar to cross off the days when you complete the task. That can help too.

Find a way to hold yourself accountable - a business bestie, business coach, accountability group, etc. Get support to get more done.

Being committed to consistency in business starts with a decision. So tell me, which reason are you guilty of?

How I deal with lack of consistency in my business?

Enter the "The Daily Five".
The Daily Five are the five core activities you MUST do in your business every day to keep you visible, earning

money and staying consistent and if that is ALL you do in a day, then you're good. When life happens, you focus on your daily five, and you can "keep the fire burning".

With my clients, I encourage them to create their daily five, and these are things that they do every day in their business to keep the consistency moving and the momentum going. If you think about a plane, train, a big piece of machinery - or anything in life really - a lot of the energy is taken up at the start to get that thing going. However, once it's moving, it's a lot easier to keep going and like with anything in life, once you're in motion, it's a lot easier to keep up the momentum.

What are the things that you're going to do in your business every single day that will keep the momentum going? One of them should be something related to visibility. One of them needs to be a sales activity, and another other should be around mindset. The other two can be whatever you want. For me, my daily five is around journaling, prayer, and spending that quiet time to reflect in my gratitude and affirmations. I also have messaging in there, which is working on getting my message out. Whether it's Facebook Live, emailing my list or posting in the CEO Mastery Group.

In terms of sales it can be just following up with people, pitching an offer, either into my group or my list. Another thing I do is track my money. It's so important to monitor that and know what's coming in and what's going out.

Then the other thing is I like to spend 15 to 20 minutes a day on is personal development. This will be either watching something, listening to something or reading something.

Being consistent in the little things will add up to help us to get that big result. Sometimes people will think, *"Oh well, I'll just do this big thing here and I'll just do this big thing again in three weeks' time and then yes, everything will be fine."* However, slow and steady does win the race.

Does it take hours to do? Nope. In fact you can be done in an hour or less once you get into the rhythm.

My Daily Five includes:
* mindset work
* visibility activity
* sales activity
* something to build my community
* creating content

Check out this 5-minute training I did on the subject >>**http://chichie.co/yourdaily5**

MINDSET + CONFIDENCE

Don't stop taking showers - the power of your mind

Success in business is 80% mindset and 20% strategy (based on the Pareto Principle) but what exactly IS mindset?

I did a quick Google search and it came back with this: *"mindset... the established set of attitudes held by someone[3]".*

So essentially it is what you believe. Our beliefs and attitudes begin to form early on in our lives and become moulded by what we see, hear and experience.

Our beliefs can either push us to do great things or limit us in achieving what we are capable of doing. These are limiting beliefs because they constrain us in some way and lead to self-limiting behaviours.

Let me give you an example.

If you believe that making money is hard, then you will expect the process of making money to be hard work. When opportunities arise, where you can easily earn or

---

[3] www.dictionary.com

receive money, you will subconsciously find a way to reject or sabotage it because your belief tells you that "making money is hard."

Where would that belief have come from? Well, maybe you heard your parents always talking about how hard it was to make money. Or perhaps you had a parent who you never saw because they were always working and you equate the money they earned to working hard and not being able to see them.

All the beliefs we currently hold are attached to some piece of evidence which supports it. Whether the idea is right or not, it comes down to identifying that theory, asking yourself whether this is true or not, seeking new evidence to support the correct belief and reprogramming your mind with the new truth.

Another one which I hear a lot and one I struggled with is *"I don't deserve this"* or *"I don't deserve to be successful"*.

For me this stemmed from being repeatedly told by various people that I wasn't good enough, I would never make it, I was wasting my time, etc.
And so that is what I believed.

Was that truth? Of course not, but if you hear something enough times and you think the source is "credible," i.e., someone who you respect or has played a key role in your life (e.g., parent/spouse), you start to believe it.

You genuinely start to believe that you are not good enough. So you stop putting yourself forward for things. You don't show up powerfully, doing the things you know you would like to do. You don't charge for your product and services appropriately. When opportunities arise you turn them down, because "it's too good to be true".

Even when you achieve success, you don't celebrate it because you feel that it is a fluke and so you sabotage yourself. And so the cycle continues.

Limiting beliefs turn into limiting behaviours.
To break this destructive chain, you have to go back to the root and ask yourself what truth is.

Do I deserve success? Why?
Am I good at what I do? Why?
In answering each of the "whys," you need to bring your evidence.

So for me I began to keep copies of any posts, emails or comments made that **supported** the belief that *I am good at what I do, I deserve to be paid for what I do, I deserve success*, and it was powerful. They are all stored in Evernote, and I can refer back to them at any time and be reminded with evidence.

I would then create affirmations around the person I *chose* to believe I was and repeated them daily, either by writing them down or by recording myself speaking them and listening on repeat.

Over time you reprogram your subconscious mind with the truth, and it is your subconscious mind which influences our behaviour.

"If you think you can do a thing or think you can't do a thing, you're right." Henry Ford.

Your success is determined by your belief. Believe in yourself, and you will succeed.

When I first started my business back in 2012, I didn't know any of this. I didn't fully understand the impact of my beliefs and how they were directly connected to my success and how I saw myself.

I knew I was good at what I did but still didn't believe in myself. This reflected in my pricing and the kind of work I took on.

WORKING ON YOUR MINDSET

1 - Know that this is a daily practice

Just because you worked on your mindset yesterday, doesn't mean it's a "one and done". Just like regularly taking showers is something we do, your mindset work is a daily practice which you need to undertake, cultivate and maintain.

Every day you affirm yourself.
Every day you rewrite your beliefs.
Every day you challenge things that are NOT the truth.

Every day. Every single day.

What would happen if you stopped taking regular showers or brushing your teeth daily? You would be a very stinky person to be around, and the same goes for your mind. You have to clear out the "dirt" daily - the negative beliefs thought patterns and lies that are currently influencing your present behaviour.

Don't stop taking showers.

2 - Identify your limiting fears and invisible scripts and deal with them

What are the things that you currently believe to be true, that are not TRUTH? I often say to my clients that your excuses are your limitations. When someone tries to give you advice or tells you what you need to do to solve your problem, what is your next response?

"Yeah but _____"

Whatever you say after the "but" is your excuse and we all have them.

For example -
Me: *So to increase your visibility I'd like you to start Live streaming as it will help build the 'know, like and trust' much quicker.*

You: *Yeah, but I don't have the right kit. No one is going to like me; people will make fun of me. I don't know how to do it; I am not trained enough, it is too hard, I don't know what to say, what if I look stupid...*

Stop fighting for your excuses and fight for your dreams.

Common excuses I hear all the time:

I don't have enough time.
I don't have enough money/influence/knowledge or connections to get started.
No one is going to take me seriously because I am too young, too old, too short, too overweight, black, a woman, from the wrong side of town, uneducated, not good enough, etc.
It's too hard.
What's the point? I'm not going to succeed anyway.
It's too late to go after my dream.

There is NO truth in any of the above statements, absolutely none. We tell ourselves these stories because we are scared.

I know this because that was me. I wanted to leave my job. I wanted to grow my business but I was afraid, and so I held myself back.

"You will get what you want when you stop making excuses about why you don't have it." - Unknown

So what's the difference between Limitations and Excuses?

A limitation is an obstacle in life. Everyone has them; yet many people still achieve success despite some huge obstacles.

Example - you're a single mum, you are building your business around your job so have less time, and maybe limited funds to build your business.

An excuse is a poor attempt to use a limitation to justify the fact that you have given up on your goal.

Example - I have no time to build my business because of my job. What is the truth in this? Find yours!

3 - Have a good morning routine
Having children taught me the importance of waking up early and having a morning routine. Whether you're a parent or not, you'll find that without it your day just STARTS and you are less productive.

Having a morning routine means that you start your day with intention and you're not running around like a headless chicken wondering how it's already 2pm and you haven't achieved anything.

I like to 'start' my day and not roll into it. I feel displaced and disorganised when that happens, and by spending 2-3 hours in the morning before the rest of my household, I can be more present during the day.

When I was in my 9-5, I knew that in order to make progress in my business I would not only need structure but a solid morning routine. I joined the '5am club' and began using the first few hours of the day to get myself and my mindset in the right place for success.

So how do you create a morning routine? Well, it's different for everyone and based on whatever your circumstances are, but an excellent book which helped me was Hal Elrod's *Miracle Morning*. Hal was in a really bad place in his life and he decided to create a morning routine for himself, and it changed his life.

In Miracle Morning, Hal uses the acronym SAVERS to walk you through the components of a good morning routine, and I have adapted this to suit me and my lifestyle.

The six areas for your morning routine are:

SILENCE

This is your opportunity to get quiet and start your day either in prayer, meditation or reflective thought. For me having a "quiet time" gives me the opportunity to think but also to listen. What is God telling me today? I can thank him for the day and ask for His guidance.

If you find that you have woken up with a million and one things running through your head, grab a piece of paper and do a brain dump. I find when I do this, I don't spend my entire morning routine thinking about my to-do list or the laundry that needs to go in the dryer.

Clear your mind from your mental clutter.

AFFIRMATIONS

I use affirmations to "speak" into my life the things I desire and want to achieve. I often write a lot of "I am" statements as well as declarations.

If you remember our earlier section on mindset, it is important to reprogram your mind for success.

Words are so powerful. The Bible says *"the power of life and death is in the tongue"*[4]. Your words have the power to bring life to a situation or destroy it, so always speak life, especially to yourself. When I learnt this, I became more aware of how I spoke to myself and others, because you can literally bring about your words.

Remember that your thoughts influence your beliefs which influence your actions.

Writing 'I AM' statements is a great way to be intentional about the things you say to yourself and speak into your future. It is something I get my clients to do, and it is really powerful.

Once you have written them, you then have the option of reading them out to yourself every day or record yourself speaking them on your phone's voice recorder and listen to your affirmations daily.

Other affirmations can be statements of things you believe to be true or want to train your subconscious to accept as

---

[4] The Holy Bible, Proverbs 18:21

true. They are also great for diffusing a situation. So, for example, you want to make a purchase, and you are worried about spending the money. One of my favourite affirmations is "I pay my bills with ease; I have enough money for all of my desires".

Inside the book bonus hub, I have an mp3 file full of affirmations that I have created so you can download.

Access it here:
http://chichie.co/ifonlytheyknewbook.

What affirmations or I AM statements can you create for yourself?

VISUALISATION
"I believe it when I see it."

This statement is truer than you realise.

When looking to create and achieve goals, if you can't picture yourself attaining it, it's going to be hard for your brain to connect you with that vision. However, if you can visualise the thing or experience you want to create, you then give your mind the opportunity to help bring it to fruition and while this might sound a bit "woo-woo," hear me out.

Neuroscience, in recent years, has determined that our subconscious brain is responsible for making most of our decisions.

The conscious, logical and rational part of our brain, the neocortex, provides input. The subconscious is the ultimate decision maker![5]

And here's the thing, the subconscious mind cannot read, it thinks only in pictures and emotions, so you can actually accelerate the results you want by spending time visualising the outcome you want!

Athletes do this all the time - they visualise the result they want, and when the time comes to perform, their mind has played out the scenario so many times that it's pretty much a done deal.

What results are you looking to achieve in your business and how can visualisation help you?

---

[5] www.neurosciencemarketing.com

One practical thing you can do, that really helped me, is to create a vision board, which is essentially pictures and words which depict the outcomes and goals that you want. Have it somewhere you can see it daily and reflect on the emotions you feel when reviewing it.

2016 was the first year that I did this and I was amazed at how I achieved almost everything on that board. I even wrote out my resignation letter, dated it and had it hanging on my wall so that I could see it every day. Nine months later I was handing in my notice - that is the power of visualisation.

Have you ever noticed that when you give your mind a problem, it sets about to figure out a solution? If you are struggling to figure something out, ask yourself the question right before you go to bed and see what happens when you wake up. For me every single time, the solution presents itself because it has been my subconscious mind doing the work in the background.

EXERCISE

Looking after yourself especially as an entrepreneur really should be a 'non-negotiable' because you are the biggest asset to your business. If anything happens to you or you get sick - depending on how you have set up your business - this could prove to be quite challenging. We all have those stories of how we push ourselves and ignore the warning signs until our body forces to rest, so to avoid that we should choose to prioritise on our health.

This includes what we eat or drink and the kind of exercise we do. Incorporate some movement into your day. If you can't do it in the morning, no problem - maybe a lunchtime walk will suffice, but decide to look after yourself.

READING

Successful CEOs are 'forever the student,' meaning that they are always learning. What was the last book you read or podcast you listened to?

I love reading as you know and tend to alternate between Kindle, a physical book and Audible, the goal being to keep "sharpening the saw" and developing myself. It also helps if you have decided to focus on a particular area and to read books in that area to develop yourself. It doesn't have to be hours on end; you can commit at least 15-mins a day to personal development and learning because this is all about consistency and doing something every day. So choose what works for you - a book, a podcast, a live stream video and commit to developing yourself every day.

SCRIBE

This is all about journaling. I use my morning routine to brain dump, set my intentions, make plans and un-clutter my mind. Some people like to journal loads, and others prefer to make it quick and concise. Do whatever works for you. In my journaling practice, I write the things I am grateful for; I set my intention for the day including how much I would like to earn/receive, I also work through any fears or challenges I am experiencing and essentially coach myself through it. Write out your goals every day. Remind yourself of what you want to achieve, get excited about achieving them.

If you have never tried journaling, I encourage you to give it a go. Don't over think and see what difference it makes.

So there you have the six areas for your morning routine. Do you have a morning routine?

4- Surround Yourself With Quality People

"You are the average of the five people you surround yourself with" - *Jim Rohn*

Selecting the right people to hang out with is probably one of the most directly important things in helping you achieve success. When I first my business five years ago, I didn't know online entrepreneurs existed. One of my friends shared with me details of a group she was in, and I was blown away. Finally, I had a community of women who understood and got me, and I felt like I was coming home!

It's really hard to build a business when you are in isolation and especially if the people around don't support or understand what you are doing and their way of "helping" is telling you to go and get a proper job. You end up questioning yourself, getting frustrated and in some cases doubting yourself so much that you walk away from your dream.

Remember that only you know the vision that God has given to you and trying to get others to buy into something they don't understand is going to leave you frustrated. Rather why not go and find *your people*. People who get you and can support you.

I have learnt that there is no point going to share certain things about my business with my non-entrepreneurial friends because this is not their space and they don't get it.

It is vital that you protect your dream because if you overshare about your business challenges (even if you do share the good stuff), that is all people will remember, and they will only encourage you to quit.

Now as you're reading this book, I can safely assume that you are not looking to quit, so choose the people you share things with wisely.

Like maybe your mastermind group, your mentor or your business BFF - people who 'get it'. They have either been where you are or are where you want to be and can give appropriate advice and guidance.

In my first year of business, I joined forces with four other women, and we formed our own mastermind.

It was one of the best things I did for my business that year because it brought five minds together and within that - aside from the support, the collaboration, the advice, etc. - it gave me a safe space to share my ideas, to cry and to grow as a businesswoman. We also were very different in our skill sets so we could help and support each other that way too.

Being in mastermind and surrounding myself with other great entrepreneurs has helped to show me what is possible and also elevate my business more than I could imagine. This is why I have programs like The Collective - because I know how isolating entrepreneurship can be. I also know how much you can grow your business, just by virtue of the people you are hanging out with.

Evaluate your circle. Who are you spending time with? Do they uplift and inspire you or bring you down. Choose wisely. Looking for a supportive community, come join the **CEO Mastery Group (www.ceomasterygroup.com)** and get the support you need there.

5 - Elevate your environment

As full-time freedom entrepreneurs, we have the luxury of working from anywhere. The bed, the kitchen table, the coffee shop. As long as there is the internet, most of us can work anywhere. Choose to and *create* environments which inspire you into action. Remove the clutter and see how it positively impacts your mind too.

This past year I created a proper home office for myself, and it made such a difference.

6 - Don't reinvent the wheel

There isn't anything new in this world. Whatever you want to achieve, I am pretty sure that there is already someone out there who has done it or has done something similar.

Success leaves clues, and a CEO does not reinvent the wheel. Take a look at those who have gone before you and see what worked and what didn't. If you can get from A to B much quicker this way, then why not, which is why I believe in having mentors who can show you the path, rather than trying to figure it out blindly.

Mentorship can be 1:1 or through their content (books like this, podcasts, live video, etc.). The important thing is the help you need is out there.

7 - Ask for help

I have learnt over the years that successful people are okay with asking for help. They recognise that they cannot do everything themselves AND they also know their strengths and focus on working solely in their zone of genius.

How do you feel about getting help or asking for support? As women, we think that we are putting people out or will look silly for asking, but again if you don't ask, you don't get. Don't suffer in silence.

8 - Say NO
Yep! Straight and simple. Sometimes the best thing you can do for yourself in a particular situation is to to JUST SAY NO. Having firm boundaries in your business is vital for helping you grow your business as well as your peace of mind.

To read more about boundaries in business, check out this article I wrote for The Guardian on this very subject.

Summary
The CEO Mindset is a choice. You decide the kind of life and business you want to have. You decide to challenge the stories that are false and create new ones.

If you are not happy with where your life is you have a CHOICE.

The power lies with you. Not anyone else. Not your partner, not your friends, not your coach - but you.

VISIBILITY AND COMMUNITY

Getting your business noticed

As business owners, letting the world know we exist is necessary for our business growth. If your potential clients don't know who you are or how you can help them, how can they buy from you?

Visibility is a new buzzword for marketing which is simply "the action or business of promoting and selling products or services, including market research and advertising."

Here are six reasons why visibility is important:
- It makes you stand out in an often crowded marketplace
- It enables you to make connections
- You can build relationships with your clients
- You can spread your message far and wide
- You are able to inspire others
- You can sign on more clients.

You need consistent visibility in order to build the know, like and trust factor, and (according to the Online Marketing Institute) it can take 7 - 13+ touches for someone to go from just meeting you to making a purchase.

The big question I hear when I talk to small business owners is *"how can I effectively market or grow my business when I don't have a big budget? There is not a lot I can do!"*

I disagree!

There is A LOT you can do and I am going to show you below, but first let me encourage you with something.

There is no such thing as an overnight success. If you're planning to be in business for the long haul, then know that the seeds you are sowing today are for a harvest in season. Marketing usually has a 90-day window for you to see real effects.
Sure, things can happen quicker, but I want to manage your expectations. Getting started is the hardest part, but once you get going all, you need to do is maintain the momentum.
Also, you need to go into this with the desire that you DO want to be more visible and you DO want to get your business noticed so that all of your actions can flow from this.

So let's get started - here are my 15 ways to get your business noticed when you don't have a big budget.

1 - Get Online
If you are running a business that still has no online presence, you need to ask yourself why.

With 40% of the world online even having a Facebook page for your business is a start (helps with SEO too) and at the very least a landing page, if you are not ready to pull together a full website. People do the majority of their internet searches and research on their mobiles, so you need to have your information readily accessible online.

Why? Because people *will* search for you.

ACTION - Not sure how to pull together a quick and easy landing page? Watch my tutorial here.

2 - Run free or low-cost workshops or training in your local community
So many organisations are looking for experts to come and train their members.
The benefits of doing it for someone else is that you don't have to worry about marketing or event costs, you just

show up and deliver. I do regular workshops for my local Enterprise organisation in person as well as online workshops for organisations such as Enterprise Nation.

In return, I get to raise my business profile locally and also welcome people into my community online.

ACTION - Which local organisation could you offer your expertise to? Shortlist your favourites and reach out to them. One way to also get into these places is to become a member and offer your help that way too. They tend to give preferences to their members.

3 - Host an in-person meet up

Living in the online space, we forget how powerful in-person connection is. Hosting a free meetup at a local coffee shop where you can also talk a little bit about what you do, is an opportunity to get your business noticed locally. You can also run paid events but bear in mind that they are not always as profitable in the short term - the effort and resources invested with these have to be weighed against the exposure you get.

ACTION - Could you host a meet up in your local area? Or maybe you can attend one that has been organised by someone else. Check out meetup.com for more details of what is available in your local area.

4 - Speak at other people's events

Do you have a strong area of expertise and feel comfortable talking in front of people? Then why not offer your services as a speaker, even smaller events are a great opportunity to raise your business profile and get new clients.

Again, many organisations are looking for good people to talk to their members/delegates and in return, you get to share your knowledge, expand your network and also build your list.

In the past year, I have spoken at industry events, churches, charity organisations, business forums, schools and more.
I find that speaking has a long-term ROI as other events and opportunities have evolved out of the events I have done, as well as new clients.

ACTION - What three topics could you comfortably talk about? Which organisations do you think would benefit from this knowledge? Time to pitch yourself.

5 - Guest blog

Guest blogging is perfect especially when you are starting out. Why? Because when you are new you have no platform and by submitting quality content to a much larger site you can get in front of their audience and build yours at the same time. It gets you noticed and known, it helps drive traffic back to your website, and if you are strategic, you can be building your email list as well.

I have guest posted for the likes of The Guardian Huffington Post, YFS, and Talented Ladies Club and they definitely helped to get my business noticed!

ACTION - Write a list of 10 publications that you know your ideal client would read, and you would like to feature in. Find out what their submission guidelines are and work your way through your list.

6 - Podcasting - Be a guest and/or start your own.

As some who prefers to talk rather than write, I love podcasting.

From a listener perspective, I really enjoy being able to learn and connect with other entrepreneurs through their podcasts and as a podcast host and someone who has been interviewed, it gives me the opportunity to get my business in front of new people who might not have heard of me before.

Now while setting up a podcast isn't 100% free (there is the kit, hosting of the audio, etc.), it is low cost and allows you to build on your expert status, reach international markets and grow your email list too, if you provide a free lead magnet.

You can check out my podcast here at www.ceomasterypodcast.com.

ACTION - Write a list of 10 podcasts that you know your ideal client would listen to and apply to be interviewed. Be sure that you are clear on your story and the value you will bring to their listeners. Tip - in iTunes, find podcasts that you like and then click on the link for similar podcasts to get access to more in the same niche.

7 - Live video

If you are looking for an impactful way to connect with your tribe, share your message and build your credibility, video does that you far quicker than any written content would.

With Facebook Live you can use your phone or computer to live stream from anywhere.

How does it get your business noticed? Well first off, Facebook love live videos so they give it higher priority in the newsfeed and more people are likely to see it. But more importantly, you now have your television show. Use it share your story, give value, teach, share and more.

Videos can very quickly go viral (one of mine did and hit 156k+ views), and with shorter attention spans, you will find people don't mind watching or listening to a video.

ACTION - Struggling with where to start with Facebook live? Grab my free guide to help you get started inside the book bonus hub - http://chichie.co/ifonlytheyknewbook

8 - Start your own Facebook or Linkedin Group

More and more people are craving connection and community. Starting your own group does not only provide both of these things, but you also increase the expert status of your business exponentially if used strategically.

As long as you don't make it about you and deliver value consistently through content you will be fine - remember it's about the community.

ACTION - Review your business model and decide whether having a community in the form of a Facebook or Linkedin group is a good idea for you. Facebook groups allow you to showcase your knowledge and connect much closer to your community. The only downside is while they cost very little in terms of money, they are very time intensive.

9 - Leverage social media

Social media is FREE.

By committing to showing up and giving value, engaging with your audience, asking questions, sharing helpful resources, you can quickly start to get your business noticed. If people to see you as a regular source of inspiration and information, they will come back and tell their friends.

Choose the platforms where you *know* your ideal client is hanging out and be there consistently.

Use tools like Smarter Queue to schedule your posts and be sure to engage and respond on a regular basis.

If your people are on Twitter, you could also consider hosting a Twitter chat as a way to raising your business profile.

ACTION - Do a social media audit. Are you on the right platforms, do you need to shut any down? How can you build more engagement and value with your existing fans?

10 - Collaborate with other business owners with complimentary services

Who do you know and who you can collaborate with? Someone who can get you in front of their audience and you in front of them? This is a great organic way to get your business noticed within new communities. You want to choose someone who has a similar audience size and host a joint workshop or even keep it simple and swap each other's freebies.

Keep your eye out for opportunities.

ACTION - What sort of businesses would be a great fit for yours? Reach out to them and see what things you can do together.

11 - Personal outreach and leveraging your networks

How many people in your network actually know what it is that you do? Like seriously? So often we think people know, but often they don't, and so you need to tell them, regularly. And also tell them the kind of people you want to work with.

ACTION - Post on your personal Facebook or Linkedin profile what you do and who you help. Send an email to your friends and family letting them know what you do and who you help and if they can refer anyone to you. If you haven't updated Linkedin, now is your time to do it!

You don't ask you don't get!

12 - Host an online summit or be part of one

Hosting a summit or online conference is a great way to get your name out there. Not only will you be known through the promotion of the event, but everyone who will be speaking at your event will also be promoting it to their networks and this will increase your reach too.

There does tend to be a lot of work involved in the run-up but done well it can really raise your visibility. An alternative is to be part of a summit, but again as these tend to be by invitation, focusing on increasing your overall visibility will help here.

ACTION - Consider whether hosting a summit is right for you.

13 - Become a guest expert

You can do this in someone else's group or as part of their program. In CEO Mastery, my free Facebook Community I give my clients the opportunity to take over the group for a day with Takeover Tuesday. This gives them the opportunity to effectively be "guest experts" on my platform.

I have also had the opportunity to be a guest expert for other people in their courses and programs.

ACTION - How can you be a guest expert? Be clear on what is it you are good at and want to become known for.

Identify communities where you feel you could add value and look to approach other leaders. Also keep an eye out for people who are looking for guests for their programs and reach out.

14 - Optimise your website

Search engine optimisation is an organic way to get your business noticed in the search engines. Through the optimisation of pages and posts - especially content that is relevant and timely to your audience - you can find yourself ranking highly for a particular search phrase.

It doesn't have to be complicated. Little things like giving your images an "alt" tag description helps them show up more in the search engines.

ACTION - If you are using WordPress be sure to install SEO by Yoast, a great plugin for helping you with on page optimisations.

15 - Leverage the press (local and otherwise)

Doing something in your local community that is worth sharing or maybe you are able to respond to a journalist request on a particular topic. Keep your eye out for ways to get yourself or your business featured. News outlets are always looking for stories that they can share.

When I ran my first local workshop, I let my local magazine know, and they printed a free feature on it!

ACTION - On Twitter look out for the hashtag #journorequest or sign up for HARO (Help A Reporter Out) for opportunities to respond to journalists on pieces they are writing.

BONUS TIPS

Write a book - like this one is sure fire way to get your business noticed. A book brings huge credibility and awareness for your business and brand. No longer do we have to wait for a traditional publisher; now you can write, self-publish and be on Amazon in a weekend.

Facebook Ads - You can start with as little as £2 a day and to help build brand awareness and eventually qualified leads. This was the strategy that I used that helped my video go viral.

Through the use of Facebook Live videos, which I boosted, I was able to retarget the video watchers with my ads for my new lead magnet which converted really well.

Facebook Ads are brilliant for reaching new and bigger audiences.

The truth about visibility if you want your business to flourish

"You've got to post 12 times a day".
"You have to live stream".
"You need to post daily pictures on Instagram and Snapchat"...

The list of 'musts' and 'must nots' when it comes to visibility online is endless and exhausting, and yet without that it, you have no business.

If people don't know you exist, how can you help them?

It wasn't until I became a coach that I had to work through my own visibility issues (remember we teach what we need to learn ourselves!) and address those fears.

What fears come up for you when you think about being more visible in your business?
Are those fears justified? Are they truth?

I had to challenge every fear I had with truth.

I quickly realised that if I want to see real success in my business, I needed to "come out of hiding" and be me.

Open myself up to be vulnerable and use my journey as a way to encourage and inspire others coming up behind me. It was okay to remove the mask.

I reconnected with my 'why' - the reason why I do the powerful work I do - and chose to believe that my message was bigger than my ego. People need to hear from you, the real you, not the Instagram filtered you.

We have to get over ourselves.

Decide and make a commitment to show up consistently.

If you are not as visible as you would like right now in your business, why? What is the fear?

As soulful creatives with big messages to share - but more importantly lives to live - we don't want to be online for the sake of it. Every interaction we have has to be meaningful and impactful, and so it is important to define what visibility means for *you*.

I teach my clients to work from a place of strength, leveraging the things that they're good at and what feels good - whether it's writing and blogging or speaking and video - and use that in that their visibility plan. Just because you see other people on video doesn't mean that you should make that your primary platform if you hate live stream (I encourage you try it at least once, but you are under no obligation). Choose what feels good and then commit to it.

When I got serious about my own visibility, one of the questions I continually asked myself was *"Why was being visible important to me? What impact would it have on my business, clients, and community, if I was able to address my fears and show up for them?"*

The answers I came back were astounding, and I realised that I was being selfish by not showing up.

I committed to daily consistency through my videos, writing and speaking.

This consistency allowed me to grow my business quickly last year and eventually make the leap out of my 9-5 a few months later.

Like an onion, your visibility has layers, and as you address one fear and reach another level, new things will appear but keep working on it because the world needs to hear from you.

True visibility starts by being visible with yourself.
#dropthemask

SYSTEMS - BUILDING A VIRTUAL TEAM OR OUTSOURCING

Building and developing the right team around you can make or break your business. Choose the wrong people, and they can destroy what you have spent years building. On the flipside, the right people - bought into your vision - can elevate and scale your business more than you could imagine.

In this section I am going to share:
* The four ways to know that you are ready to start outsourcing
* The key benefits of outsourcing
* How to figure out what to outsource in your business
* Where to find people
* What to consider before, during and after hiring your team

So what do I mean when I talk about outsourcing and virtual teams?

Outsourcing is essentially obtaining products and services from an outside supplier.

Virtual teams or virtual assistants are people who help support your business in a variety of functions but are location independent. So right now on my team, I have different people across the world who work on various projects. We are connected through the internet, have regular meetings through video conference and collaborate in real time via cloud software.

This is the new way of doing business.

Virtual Assistants can cover anything from admin, social media, graphics, customer support, etc. The main thing here is that the role is a virtual position.

When talking with clients and other business owners, the three common reasons I hear from people as to why they haven't started outsourcing yet is that they are "not ready", "can't afford it" or "I can do it faster myself".

If you're not earning a lot of money in your business, it might feel counter-intuitive to go then and invest in additional team members. However, the reality of this is not true.

If you have a desire to grow and scale your business, you are actually limiting your growth potential by trying to do everything yourself.

When it comes to the money bit, look at this way - how much extra money are you able to make now by yourself if you have no more available hours? Additional support will allow you to you release some of that workload and begin to focus on the high-value activity in your business.

When I went from having a virtual assistant for five hours per month to ten hours per week, that produced a huge shift in my business and mindset in terms of what I was able to now release and the income I was now freed up to generate. It is no surprise I was able to leave my job four months later!

And finally when it comes to the old excuse of *"I can do it much quicker"* - yes maybe you can. But for how much longer and what are you sacrificing to complete this task? In the beginning, you will probably have to spend time training someone, but once they get it, you have your time back.

So how do you know when you are ready to start outsourcing? Here are four key signs:

1. You have run out of capacity. There are so many hours in the day, and if you're finding yourself working 80-hour weeks and things are still not getting finished, it's time to evaluate what you're doing in your business and whether you are the best person to do that task.
2. It is a task you are not able to do. Rather than spend hours trawling through Google and Youtube, trying to figure it out yourself, pay someone who is an expert to do it for you, and they complete it far quicker.
3. It is a task you don't like to do. There are some things we just don't like doing in our business, but yet are important activities, which if we neglect can have a detrimental impact. For me, that is invoicing, chasing up payments, etc. If you feel the same about certain activities, outsourcing them is then the way to go.
4. You want to grow and scale your business. As I said above, you can only do so much when it's just you. Bringing in additional support helps to free up more time and create more opportunities for you in your business. You are also supported more

in your business and can create better workflows, synergies, and efficiencies.

As the CEO in your business, you need to know where to focus your time and energy for maximum return. Low-level admin tasks should not be replacing high-value marketing and sales activities which are high priority for any business.

You will know what the high-value tasks are, but too often you are unable to spend your time doing them because you are bogged down with the low level activities which you *should* outsource.

The first task I outsourced in my business were social media, website/WordPress work, and admin tasks. I went through a number of different people before I found someone who was reliable and she stayed with me for a year.

So if you decide that it's time to hire someone, where do you even start?

Well I recommend that you spend time getting clear on what your overall vision and goals are for your business.

From there you can start to design what your business will look like in terms of the various tasks and roles.

Next, you identify the tasks you want to outsource. To help you do this, you want to create what Chris Ducker calls <u>*"Three Lists to Freedom"*</u>.

* Things you hate doing every day
* Things you can't do
* Things you shouldn't be doing

Item three is the game changer because so many us are doing things we shouldn't be doing, even if it is something we enjoy.

And just because you *can* do something, doesn't mean that you should.

Take these identified tasks, and start to pull together a job description or project outline for what you want help with. You want to create a clear job description so that you can confidently go out recruiting, knowing what you are looking for.

My top places are to find freelancers/contractors:

Your Community

My current assistant is a member of my free Facebook group, and when I posted that I was looking for an assistant, she applied. I had never thought about reaching out to my community, but the benefits are huge. These are people who have already bought into your brand and more often than not, are excited at the opportunity to get involved.

Courses and Programs you are taking or other paid groups

My best VA to date was a girl I met on a group coaching program. I liked her attitude and personality inside the Facebook group, and when she announced she was starting up a VA business I approached her about working together, and she was with me for nine months.

Free Facebook Groups

I am part of a number of what I call "professional" Facebook groups, i.e., they are tailored to specific industries.

Search for Virtual Assistant Groups on Facebook and search for people there. Be warned you WILL get inundated with posts when people apply.

Referrals

Who do you know? Who do the people you know, know? Ask around but remember to do your due diligence still. Just because someone is referred does not mean that they are perfect or without fault. Still, ensure that they are the right person for the job.

Upwork

Great for one-off jobs or specific things if the above are not options for you. Price and experience varies, but this is where I started and had a few good experiences and some not so good ones too!

The Interview Process

I like to connect with prospective candidates through Skype initially - we chat and then have a conversation. I am interested in understanding their background and experience, why they want to work for me, what they can bring to the table and anything that might have an impact on their work including time zone conflicts.

For example, some of my team members are mums which means they effectively work flexi-time (aka any free time they have), now this is not a problem for me (I have two kids of my own), as long as the work gets done when it is due. But knowing that I have a team member that has children gives me context to their working environment and expectations.

Once I am happy with the interview process, I give them a real piece of work from my business to complete. I do this for many reasons. I want to validate their experience claims, but I also want to see what it is like working with them, how they communicate and react in different situations - oh so important.

Once that job is complete and I'm happy with the outcome, they come onboard properly as part of the team, which includes contract, NDA (Non-Disclosure Agreement) and a welcome pack (which includes their job description and a personal welcome from me).

Ongoing Support and Team Building

Managing a remote team can be challenging. Communication is key both individually and as a team on the whole. It is important to connect with your team on a regular basis - I meet each of my team members weekly. In between those sessions, we communicate via Slack and manage our projects via Asana.

Each team member also has KPIs (key performance indicators) which are targets we have agreed together and track in their 1:1 sessions.

It is important to note that building a team is as much about the people as it is you being a good leader. There will be challenges, so it is important that you are clear on your values and boundaries. Also, know that this is business and nothing is personal, or at least it shouldn't be, hence why having clear objectives and KPIs removes any emotional elements from work conversations.

Final tips

* Be clear on your overall vision for your business and where this role fits in

* Advertise for the role and not the title, e.g., I need someone to assist me with creating a new landing page in Clickfunnels and webinar sequence, rather than I need a Techie VA
* Decide on what things are important to you for the role - location, experience, cost, etc.

* SOP the heck out of your business, i.e., get your systems in place and create Standard Operating

Procedures. This continues to be a work in progress as my business continues to grow, however bringing in team members forced me to get organised in this area, from what tools we use right through to the actual steps we take to do a particular activity. The benefit of this is that you stop being the block in your business and other team members can help each other out

* Be clear on expectations from both sides

* Cultivate strong communication throughout the process and when working together

* Give them a test project before moving into a retainer

* The right team can propel your business forward so much and so use the tips above to ensure that you get the right people first time round.

MONEY MASTERY

Being able to manage your money and cash flow as an entrepreneur is the difference between success and being out of business.

How Not To Get Yourself In A Hole

Wednesday, July 5th, 2017; Facebook:
Just got off the phone with my accountant.

The importance of being close to your numbers cannot be overestimated.

This is not an area of strength for me but is something I am working hard to become better at.

For years I have battled with personal debt, constant overspending and mismanagement and I realised that to be successful I need to take responsibility and get a better handle on it.

It's all good to focus on sales, but if you neglect cash flow, tax and profit you can very nearly destroy your business.
Trust me when I say this. I speak from experience.
So today we discussed:
- income goals
- VAT registration (yes it is coming this summer)
- planning my launches and pricing to align with goals
- making sure I know my tax numbers and I am planning for them
- how I invoice and making sure I am using the right tools

- bookkeeping because I realise it is time to take this off my hands

MONEY MISTAKES THAT I HAVE MADE THAT YOU DON'T HAVE TO

1. Not tracking my numbers and keeping poor records
I now use Quickbooks which is synced to my bank account and PayPal, so all my transactions are logged and reconciled. No more guessing or wondering. You can keep things simple and use a spreadsheet or pen and paper. The main thing is to keep good records and be consistent with recording your information.

2. Not putting money aside for tax
I have a separate savings account for tax savings and soon to be VAT. Nothing worse than scrambling around to find money to pay the tax man. It is the WORST. Get prepared and plan for it.

3. Ignoring affordability
Not keeping track of expenses and spending in my business without checking the business could actually afford it. Get the book Profit First by Mike Michalowicz. Read it. Implement.

I regularly review what I am spending in my business and cancel subscriptions and payments I no longer need or use. Check this quarterly for yourself. PayPal automatic payments are the worst. Go in and cancel those bad boys.

4. Focusing on revenue (which is important) rather than profitability (key).

Everyone likes to shout about revenue, but I've learnt that this is only one half of the equation. You can be earning all this money and spending it all, and you'll end up broke and with no profit.

For an online business especially, the goal of profit should be a priority as our overheads are practically non-existent.

After all is said and done - what is your profit?

5. Not realising the importance of cashflow

Cash is king, so being able to project and know what is coming in and out of your business to see if you have enough to pay for things is key. I learnt the hard way and had periods when I couldn't pay my team on time. It wasn't good, and I vowed never to be in that place again, so now I make cashflow a priority.

6. Burying my head in the sand rather than seeking help

This is the worst. Shame, embarrassment are all things that you feel when you are dealing with financial issues. But the worst thing you can do is hide away. Silence is a killer, and you can't get help if people don't know what is going on. So be brave, reach out, tell people what is going on, you will be surprised at the positive response you get.

7. Ignoring the importance of money mindset and how it is a continuous practice

Reading books on wealth and money mastery, practicing gratitude and having an abundance mindset help to keep things in check.

So over to you.

Do you know your numbers? Do you track your numbers? Is your business profitable? Are your expenses in check?

What changes do you need to make?

FINAL THOUGHTS

23 BUSINESS LESSONS - THINGS I HAVE LEARNT

I have been in business for over 5 years and September 23rd is my business anniversary, here are 23 lessons I have learnt along the way.

1. This business journey is a marathon, not a sprint, so don't compare someone else's seven-year journey to your six-month one. Acknowledge where you are at and be grateful for it. Also be open to your business evolving as you grow.
2. Just like in a marriage, you will learn more about yourself than you imagine. Running a business brings up all the fears, beliefs and stories you have ever told yourself. And the great thing is you get to rewrite them.
3. Clients will amaze you. Clients will hurt you. Know that whatever happens it's never normally about you.
4. Create your own cheerleading squad, your support network because here's the thing - not everyone will get you or support you. Don't spend time trying to convince them. Believe in yourself.
5. Trust your intuition always, it's never wrong.
6. Self-belief and self-trust are the cornerstone of everything.

7. What got you here, will not get you there. Constantly be reviewing things and switching things up. Never stop learning.
8. It's okay to be scared, but take action through the fear. It's never as bad as you think.
9. Clarity comes through action. You need to implement what you know.
10. Business is personal. Whatever you are dealing with personally, will show itself in your business, so deal with your issues.
11. You need a vision. You need goals. There will never be a perfect time, so start today.
12. Invest in yourself, whether it is tools or mentors. Get clear on what you need *right now* and get that. Avoid the bright shiny objects. They will leave you broke and overwhelmed.
13. Choose mentors who understand your path, are where you want to be and can keep you accountable. Don't follow the hype.
14. Follow the results. Will your coach help you get the results you want? That's vital, but also know that no coach is the magic pill for your problems - you still have to do the work.
15. Take care of your finances from day one and they will take care of you.

16. Outsource before you are ready and watch your business grow.
17. Business is about relationships. Relationships are formed by humans. Be human. Be kind. Treat others how you would like to be treated.
18. Be yourself, not a version of someone else. Know that you are in fact competition proof and despite what you may believe, have a special something about you.
19. Define what success means to you and go after that. Ignore what others are doing. Create your business model, decide how you want to business and be unapologetic about it.
20. Embrace your story and own it. Somebody needs to hear it.
21. Don't chase the money, but respect it. Do the things that excite you, motivate you and watch the money come.
22. Know that confidence comes from consistency, commitment, and clarity.
23. Stay in your lane. Always.

FINAL WORDS- NOTE FROM CHICHI

Thank you for spending this time with me and sharing my journey. I am by no means finished with this adventure - I am learning every day, as I know you are.

The day a person stops learning and giving, they start dying, and I truly believe that you've read this book today because you want to keep *growing*. That tells me something about you - that you will succeed.

You've taken that first step.

You've identified that you need help to hit the levels you know you're capable of.

You've invested in yourself and you've shown up today because you have big dreams and limited time. Because you're ready to create your OWN strategy for success.

You're ready to stop talking and start doing, becoming the CEO – Consistently Executing at every Opportunity.

Yes, I see you. I believe in you.

The best is yet to come.

You've got this.

#progressoverperfection

http://chichie.co/ifonlytheyknewbook

ENJOYED THE BOOK

If you have enjoyed reading this book, please help spread the word by doing the following:

Recommend it. Suggest this book to your friends, or buy it as a gift for someone.

Talk about it. Mention it on Facebook, Twitter, Instagram etc

Create a conversation about it, using the hashtag #IfOnlyTheyKnewBook. You can write about it or review it on your blog, vlog or platform. Feel free to use the cover image on social networking sites.

Review it. Please leave a review on **Amazon UK** or **Amazon USA**. It's really easy to do and it helps other people find the book.

I love hearing from my readers and community, so please feel free to get in touch.

You can reach me at:

Email: hello@chichieruchalu.com
Website: www.chichieruchalu.com
Facebook: www.facebook.com/chichieruchaluonline
Facebook Group:www.ceomasterygroup.com
Twitter: www.twitter.com/chichieruchalu
Instagram: www.instagram.com/chichieruchalu
LinkedIn: https://www.linkedin.com/in/chichieruchalu/

THE COLLECTIVE

The Collective
CEO MASTERY MASTERMIND
JOIN NOW

Running a business was never meant to be a lonely journey.

Trying to figure things out, constantly googling and not knowing what is the best option to take.

Late nights
Early mornings

Scrolling through the Facebook newsfeed, again.

Feeling bad about all the things everyone else is doing, rather than focusing on your own amazing business.

You are determined to make your business a success and are willing to do whatever it takes.

Your non-entrepreneur friends don't get it and when you have a win, you would love to be able to get more than a "that's nice" in response.

It doesn't have to be that way.

What if you had a place where you could ask questions and get support from a group of like-minded, focused and committed women.

A place where you received solid training and guidance.
A place where you can show up, be yourself and GROW at the same time.
A place to receive mentorship.

Introducing…**The Collective**

This is my paid mastermind community for women who want to create results in their business AND life.

You want community and you want a sisterhood and support from a mentor who can guide you on your journey.

A community for women who are ready to stop:
– hiding
– making excuses
– doing it alone

And are ready to take action, every single day.

Maybe you are starting your business or maybe you're a few years in, what I know is that you are craving connection and clarity and you will get that inside The Collective.

Inside the Collective we focus on:
– consistency
– community– connection
– commitment

We say no to:
– competition

– comparison
– complaining

We know that the life we want to create for ourselves is available to us, as long as we are prepared to go after it.

To find out more visit:
http://www.chichieruchalu.com/the-collective/

Use the special code "BOOKBONUS" to receive a special price for your first month.

ABOUT THE AUTHOR

Chichi Eruchalu is a Business Strategist, Speaker and Coach who helps you overcome your fears around being seen online, so that you can show up with intention and connect with the people who need to hear from you.

Her sweet spot is business visibility, showing you how to own your gifts and leverage your strengths so that you can create an impact, not only in your life, but the lives of those around you.

She successfully made the leap from employee to entrepreneur in 2016, leaving her corporate bank job, and has since founded CEO Mastery, a global online community of over 4000 women who are empowered to create full-time freedom for themselves.

IPSE Freelancer of the Year 2017 Runner Up, she has been published in The Guardian and Huffington Post and is a Go and Grow Online Advisor for Enterprise Nation.

Chichi is passionate about helping women flourish in business and does this through her live trainings, CEO Mastery Podcast and courses.

"If Only They Knew" serves to help and inspire women into action, helping them step out courageously, building success on their own terms.

A lover of Kindle and Netflix, she lives in London with her husband and two children.

LET'S CONNECT

Website: **www.chichieruchalu.com**
Facebook: **www.fb.com/chichieruchaluonline**
Facebook Group: **www.ceomasterygroup.com**
Twitter: **www.twitter.com/chichieruchalu**
Instagram: **www.instagram.com/chichieruchalu**
LinkedIn: **www.linkedin.com/in/chichieruchalu**
YouTube: **www.chichieruchalu.com/youtube**
Podcast: **www.ceomasterypodcast.com**
Media Page: **www.chichieruchalu.com/media/**
Viral Video: **chichie.co/7-reasons-broke**

Interested in working together?
Book your complimentary
consult:www.chichieruchalu.com/chat/

REFERENCES

Books:

* What Got You Here Won't Get You There: How successful people become even more successful (Marshall Goldsmith, 2009)
* Letting Go of Stuff: Powerful Secrets to Simplify Your Life (Darren L. Johnson, 2005)
* The Miracle Morning: The Not-So-Obvious Secret Guaranteed To Transform Your Life (Hal Elrod, 2012)

Websites:

* www.chrisducker.com/3-lists-to-freedom/
* www.onlinemarketinginstitute.org
* www.theguardian.com
* www.neurosciencemarketing.com/blog/articles/subconscious-decision.htm
* www.digitalmarketer.com/lead-magnet-ideas-funnel/

Chichi's material:

* Bonus hub: http://chichie.co/ifonlytheyknewbook
* The Collective: www.facebook.com/groups/ceomasterycollective/
* On Self Care: www.chichieruchalu.com/009-sleep-not-overrated-self-care-tips/
* The end of 9-5 life: www.chichieruchalu.com/last-day-9-5

Printed in Great Britain
by Amazon